## ABOUT THE AUTHOR

Born in India of missionary parents and educated in boarding schools in India and the UK, I went on to train as a nurse at a London Teaching Hospital where I met my husband. We worked for twelve years in rural Africa in a medical missionary capacity. On returning to the UK in 1988 I later embarked on four years of training in psychodynamic counselling. We are currently based in Essex, where I work as a counsellor and supervisor in private practice and within the community. My love of the natural world facilitates interests that include walking, gardening and photography, alongside an enjoyment of family life.

*With best wishes*

*Carol.*

# FACES OF ANGER

# FACES OF ANGER

Carol Bulkeley

ATHENA PRESS
LONDON

FACES OF ANGER
Copyright © Carol Bulkeley 2004

All Rights Reserved

No part of this book may be reproduced in any form
by photocopying or by any electronic or mechanical means,
including information storage or retrieval systems,
without permission in writing from both the copyright
owner and the publisher of this book.

ISBN 1 84401 364 2

First Published 2004 by
ATHENA PRESS
Queen's House, 2 Holly Road
Twickenham, TW1 4EG
United Kingdom

Printed for Athena Press

*With Gratitude
to Mike, whose dying ultimately gave me life,
and Alan, whose therapeutic skill enabled me to increasingly discover
what that means.*

# *Acknowledgements*

As I was thinking about this, I came across an interesting comment from Anton Obholzer, Consultant psychiatrist and psychoanalyst, and Chief Executive of the Tavistock and Portman clinics, London, who in the Foreword for Neville Symington's book, *The Making of a Psychotherapist* (Karnac, 1996) wrote:

> 'Like many a creative writer Neville Symington had trodden a long and interesting path… I have often thought a certain sense of social dislocation is a requirement for being a social scientist – be it a psychotherapist, psychoanalyst, psychologist or whatever – the experience of dislocation giving a capacity to stand outside the system and to observe it with a degree of immunity to group pulls.'

In order to write as I have, it became necessary for me to 'stand outside the system'. A process that necessarily evolved gradually over a long period of time, and during which a great many people played significant roles. To each of you I am grateful.

I wish to make particular mention of my husband, who has supported me unstintingly and given endless practical help in getting my thoughts organised within a computer! Likewise our two sons, who have been supportive of the project from its earliest days.

I also wish to thank David Moore, Director of Publications and the staff at Athena Press, who have enabled publication to become a reality. Their interactions with me throughout the publication process have been marked by courtesy and respect.

To you all I say a heartfelt thank you for your belief in me.

October 2004

# *Preface*

I owe an enormous debt to the literary world for making other peoples' discoveries and creative thinking accessible to me. At a stage in my life when I have on occasions felt isolated on the path my personal journey has required me to walk, books have been wonderful companions along the way, providing timely nourishment as needed.

Whilst what I have written is mostly my own, inevitably my thoughts have been influenced and informed by what I have read from others. The text is supported by quotations from other literary sources, which I have acknowledged. However, I wish to make particular mention of the Anglican priest HA Williams, whose writing has had a profound impact upon me. Three of his books, *The True Wilderness*, *True Resurrection*, and *True to Experience* have been read again and again. I found a certain kindred spirit with him; his questioning mind that refused to be satisfied with anything less than answers that resonated authentically within the depths of his soul, and at times his frustration with elements about the institutional church, which far from facilitating freedom in relationship with God, seemed sometimes to militate against it. As I reflected on the stuck but angry position that many, including myself found ourselves in with regard to our relationship with the Church, the thought occurred that it could be helpful to share some of these discoveries. I hope that something in the pages that follow will be instrumental in freeing you to enjoy God in your own way, whether that be within the Church or outside it. Whilst no two people can ever experience the same journey, I discovered from Harry Williams' writing, that psychoanalysis had been an important feature of that journey, as it has in mine. He sadly has now died, but his wisdom and integrity live on. Authentic thought, it seems, has a power to engage and feed the soul, suggesting that we are all hungry for what Harry Williams referred to as 'inside truth'.

Inside truth as I have discovered it is what I share with you in the pages that follow. I have increasingly come to understand the profound impact we all have on one another, which, like ripples in a pond, radiate outwards in ever widening circles. In these days of appalling global conflicts it is perhaps more significant than we have adequately realised to attend to our own conflicts. The more we are able to process and resolve within ourselves, the less need is there for it to get projected and displaced elsewhere. Could this have potential for resolving conflicts on the international scene? That is a question that could have very far-reaching repercussions. On a much smaller scale we see the implications of this within families, and the very significant benefits when feelings can be owned by individual members of a family rather than displaced. How much more could such a concept influence the global scene? Questions that require much thought. I hope that this book might serve as an element in that thought process, and stimulate thought and reflection, that will bear fruit not only in your own life, but also in those whose lives overlap with yours.

June 2004.

# Contents

| | |
|---|---|
| Acknowledgements | ix |
| Preface | xi |
| Introduction | 15 |
| Context | 22 |
| The Body | 37 |
| Faces of Anger | 56 |
| Creative Anger | 91 |
| Anger and Sexuality | 113 |
| Conclusion | 129 |

## *Introduction*

The idea for this book was conceived on holiday whilst reclining on a sunbed on the southern shores of Cyprus. It was the seventeenth anniversary of the sudden and shocking death of my brother Mike in a cycling accident. He had been out with his family one damp Sunday afternoon, cycling along a quiet road alongside a reservoir, when he was hit by a speeding car. That event changed the course of several lives, including my own. Seventeen years on from that fateful day, I found myself on this particular Sunday morning reflecting on all that had happened in the intervening years, not least that in the course of my own personal journey I had painfully and with much agony of soul come to the realisation that I was no longer comfortable in the institutional Church; and for various reasons I had felt it necessary to leave. It had become an empty wineskin that no longer satisfied.

Prior to making the momentous decision to leave the Church, I had wrestled with my dissatisfaction and questioned why I continued to go, but felt incapable of leaving. Finally I had the courage to follow the dictates of my soul and do what had to be done if I were to be true to my calling and to what I perceived to be the prompting of God from within myself. It is perhaps shocking for some to imagine that I felt God was asking me to leave the Church, when the Church spends so much time and energy trying to persuade people to join. But that is how it was and believe me, it caused shockwaves, inside and out! The very fact that there is this sense of needing to persuade people to be part of the Church is an interesting dynamic. Is there a fear that without our persuasion they wouldn't be interested? Certainly it leaves little room for the creative spirit of God to prompt a person at a time in their lives when perhaps they are receptive to such things.

The sense of shock experienced primarily by me when I

decided to leave is difficult to describe. I, who all my life had 'fitted in' to please others, was now at the centre of a storm of astonishment and disapproval. I lost my church family, which was very important to me, I lost friends, I lost status as I was in a leadership position – I felt as if I had lost everything, but in fact I had gained my soul and ultimately that is what matters. And part of how I gained my soul was that through all the grief that followed this momentous step, I found myself. My real self that is, rather than the compliant false self that had built up over many years of unwittingly pleasing others and unconsciously shaping my behaviour to bring about approval from others. I was plunged deeper into my own journey of discovery and came to realise what many who have walked this way will know; that grief strips us of so much that is false as we come to discover what we really think and feel, rather than all the oughts and shoulds of how we think we should feel, which years of fitting in had trained me to do. Fitting in can be very reassuring but it is not always authentic, and sooner or later truth has a way of making us listen. It was King David in his profoundly moving lament to God for his regrettable adultery with Uriah's wife Bathsheba, who in Psalm 51:6 recognised that 'sincerity and truth are what you require' as an integral part of coming to terms with ourselves as we are.

My heart knew I could speak with God directly and allow Him to nourish me in the ways I needed, but years of earlier conditioning kept me bound to old patterns, along with a huge fear of what others would think. I remember one holiday in Majorca agonising with God over this very issue as I paddled along the water's edge one Sunday morning. Sundays for several years never failed to activate guilt and conflict about the position I found myself in. Conflicted about my inability to find nourishment within the Church, yet hugely guilty about such a situation. To my rescue came words from the Gospels: 'Why do you eat that which is not bread?' In other words, why do you persistently feel you have to swallow that which doesn't satisfy and nourish? Why, indeed? I felt God was inviting me to trust Him to nourish me and was enormously encouraged.

By this stage, even though we had left the Church, I was still under the illusion that we must immediately find another one, despite the fact that we had tried several and all of them at that time in our lives had left us with this feeling of dissatisfaction. Eventually the penny dropped that if we were meant to be in another church, it would feel right and we really didn't have to spend all this energy in 'looking for the right one'. With that realisation we stopped searching and began to relax in our new setting outside the Church as opposed to inside it. Of course there are a lot of other issues about the need to find the right one which in itself can be a trail that persistently leads one up a blind alley, but I'll not linger on that here! From our different position, and a growing sense that this was necessary and the place we were meant to be at this point in our lives, we began to view things from a wider perspective. It feels important to acknowledge that in this process of journeying, what or where one feels comfortable at any given time has always to be open to the possibility of further change. But for us at that time, the greater distance allowed us to see things that perhaps we could not have seen whilst being so immediately immersed in the life of the Church. Distance often gives a broader perspective.

This shift in position of course opened up all kinds of new possibilities. Not least the freedom to enjoy God without all the extra demands which life within the Church can sometimes generate, particularly if you are compelled by inner pressures to comply, fit in, please others by doing whatever they want and being generally unable to say no. It was a way of life which for me became a burden that was slowly but surely stifling me. I felt I was dying inside. Increasingly, I couldn't be myself and felt there was this huge pull to fit in, toe the line and not rock the boat. Alas my leaving did rock the boat, not least the boat that was my life. Philip Richter and Leslie Francis in their book about Church leavers interviewed numerous people who for one reason or another had left the Church. This particular couple said of their experience: 'The pressure is off, that pressure of belonging, doing the right thing, having the right experience has gone and it's ...absolutely liberating!'[1] The sense of liberation didn't follow immediately for me. I was heartbroken. But out of the turbulence and pain, treasures have emerged that I could never have imagined, and now several years on I can echo that sense of liberation.

As I sat in that beautiful garden on that November morning in Cyprus and reflected on my personal journey thus far, I felt deeply thankful, even if at times I still miss the sense of belonging that the Church gave me, and the status and security it provided. I realised painfully the meaning of those words of Jesus, 'What does it profit a man to gain the whole world and lose his own soul.'[2] At the point when I had to leave before any more damage was done, I was well aware the Church world was mine for the asking, with the lure of leadership, promotion in the wider denomination, the love of so many people and mine for them. I recalled the lure of the mountain-top temptation when we are told Jesus was shown all the kingdoms of the world, which could be his if he compromised his integrity. I took strength from His example and eventually made what at the time felt like an agonising decision to give up the lure of the very things I had worked so hard to achieve – and, it has to be said, still wanted! It was a decision I do not now regret, even if at times in all the turmoil that followed, I wondered whether it was worth the repercussions. I sat on the fence of indecision for a very long time, until one day various things fell into place and I knew, and with that sense of knowing came the strength to do what had to be done.

The decision was made, though not without an immense struggle, which plunged me as a result into a depth of grief that was not easy to bear. However, angels in various forms did come to my aid and in the months and years that have followed I have thought a great deal about the many who feel trapped and therefore angry regarding their Church situation, as they try to balance authentic spirituality with the demands of religious expectation, which don't always complement each other. Inevitably the conflict this can create generates angry frustration, which, if it is not resolved creatively, can end up stifling growth rather than facilitating it. 'None of us can grow any faster than our image of God,' write Mathew, Sheila and Dennis Linn in their book, *Healing Religious Addiction*.[3] For many of us our image of God has needed to develop and expand alongside the growth of a more elastic and flexible wineskin to contain the discoveries we make. It may be for some, as it was for me, that they are unaware at a conscious level how angry they are, having long since learnt to bury all such feelings. Our bodies often pay the price communicating our unease for us, whilst for others it gets taken out on their nearest and dearest. I remember our younger son when he was a teenager remarking, with the ability teenagers have to see through things, that he wondered why we went to church because we always came home so angry!

This book will not in general be a sharing of the particulars of the journey that has brought me thus far, other than to give a context out of which such changed thinking has arisen. Each of us can only share authentically those things that we have learnt and discovered for ourselves; otherwise they become the empty words and 'clanging symbols' that St Paul speaks of in his letter to the Corinthian Church,[4] which are the fruits of operating out of duty rather than love, such as when we say one thing but think something entirely different. Such words are painful to listen to, discordant and with a phoney feel about them, probably because that's what they are. They seem to lack authenticity. The things I write are the product of much soul searching and I hope will reflect that authenticity for which we are all hungry. Within the context of my life, things have happened which have caused me to think and reflect deeply, and what emerges is the fruit of having made these things my own, often agonisingly slowly, or so it has felt. Although in the overall scheme of things, what is a day?

To return to the genesis of this book. On that particular Sunday morning in Cyprus, my mind wandering from this thought to the next, I found myself revelling in my surroundings. I was in a beautifully watered garden, surrounded with hibiscus and bougainvillea, the sound of the sea yards from my feet, sunshine and blue skies above, just enjoying being. In an ecstasy of joy I exclaimed, 'this is my idea of celebrating Sunday!' I felt deeply peaceful as I communed with God in my heart, and so thankful that however stressful and demanding the journey thus far had at times been, for this moment there was the capacity to enjoy God in my own way and know that was very much okay. Not least I knew that it was not essential for me to attend a bricks-and-mortar establishment for spiritual succour and nourishment. I am reminded of what the Celtic writer David Adam wrote:

> For those who are willing to make the journey to the edges, the world and anything in it can still be the primary scripture; that which speaks to us of God. Before any books were written, God spoke through his creation, he revealed himself through the things of the earth. The signs were there for those who learned to read them. These signs are still there. But as with the written scriptures we have to learn to read and meditate on what is before us. So many of us are illiterate when it comes to reading our own environment. If only our eyes are opened to see and read, there is a fantastic depth to our lives and to every created thing; all things shine with the numinous.[5]

That morning I had an experience of meeting God through his creation which nourished me in a way which I experienced less and less within the Church. More often than not in recent years I had come away feeling dissatisfied, though unable to exactly know why. However, on those beautiful occasions when I heard the Word of God coming through a preacher who had made it his own and shared that with us, rather than a sharing of second-hand discoveries, I found myself engaged and nourished. All of which I eventually came to see was telling me that what I was hungry for was authentic spirituality that could accept differing approaches to what was helpful. The endless repetition of this commentary, or that book somehow left me feeling disappointed. Such resources obviously have their place to stretch and inform the mind, but can never be regurgitated in what at times felt an unthought-through way. What we read has to be digested if we are to make it useful to ourselves, and only then will it be useful and digestible for others. I rather think the Apostle Paul had grasped this concept when in those familiar words, now used at every communion service, he said, 'For I received from the Lord, the teaching that I passed on to you: that the Lord Jesus on the night he was betrayed…'[6]

We have first to receive it from God, and make it our own, before we can pass it on meaningfully to others. In this business of authenticity and genuineness, second-hand goods cannot compare with what we discover first hand. I realised that what I was hungry for was authenticity and integrity, which will necessarily embrace struggle as a legitimate part of that process.

In my musings that Sunday morning, I found myself

reflecting on the many who feel trapped and therefore angry about their relationship with the Church, for whom it could perhaps be quite helpful to explore some of the issues around the many faces of anger, which seems to be something of a pariah within communities of all kinds, from which the Church is no exception. At the very least the reader would know their experience was a shared experience even if the particulars might be different, and at best something within the pages that follow might set off a train of thought that could be liberating in some way. I therefore determined to write and with that started to commit my thoughts to paper.

Anger is such a creative, life-giving emotion when we are able to value and harness its energies; a resource within each of us, that can contribute significantly in bringing us to life. Yet somehow, sadly, its repression and denial through fear has had the effect of stifling life and vitality in ourselves and our communities, causing untold suffering and unhappiness, and not infrequently provoking conflicts that can when unresolved have such devastating repercussions, personally, corporately and globally.

My hope is that the writing of this book will open the door for this emotion to be embraced as a valid part of each of us, and in so doing open us in increasing measures to a fullness of life that is the inheritance of us all. Joy and pain, like night and day, belong together, though most of us need to remind ourselves of that truth at regular intervals. But before we look in more detail at the many faces of anger, I feel it could be helpful to share the context from which much of my thinking evolved. If you like, the context was the crucible within which my thinking developed.

---

NOTES

[1] Philip Richter/Leslie Francis, *Gone but not Forgotten*, Darton, Longman and Todd, 1998, p.61
[2] Mathew 16:26
[3] Matthew, Sheila and Dennis Linn, *Healing Religious Addiction*, Darton, Longman and Todd, 1995, p.37
[4] 1 Corinthian 13:1
[5] David Adam, *Border Lands*, SPCK, 1991
[6] 1 Corinthians 11:23

## Context

A crisis in my relationship with the Church served as the catalyst for me to question what I was experiencing and the effect it was having on me and others. This necessitated a great deal of thinking – and rethinking – about much that I had hitherto accepted as 'gospel', but which on further examination of what was written and implied seemed far removed from the rigid and unyielding position that my Church experience had hitherto led me to believe, and which I had unwittingly accepted. It is perhaps timely at this point to note that the meaning of the word *gospel* is good news. Much of what I had swallowed felt like anything but good news. Like the story of the Emperor's new clothes, what I was seeing with freshly opened eyes did not match what I was hearing and being expected to accept, nor could my interpretation of scripture and the character of God as I understood Him to be, sit comfortably alongside this rather demanding, tyrannical God. I now realise that many of the expectations I felt about how one ought to be emanated from that rather persecutory element within myself, but nevertheless the community also fed this with, for example, the expectation that one should attend church twice on Sunday if one were committed. Committed to whom, I found myself asking? And what was so significant about twice? I realise this has its roots in Victorian times so that servants of the household could attend church after their chores were done, yet has now in some circles become 'gospel'. It amused me that the African church, which we were a part of for many years, only ever met once on Sunday! It seems a classic illustration of the kind of thing Jesus may have been thinking when he quoted Isaiah whilst addressing some religious experts from Jerusalem, who were complaining about some of the followers of Jesus who didn't wash their hands in the proper way before they ate: 'It is no use for them to worship me, because they teach man-made rules as though they were my laws,' said Jesus.[7] I increasingly began to think a lot of things were getting laid at God's feet, and therefore claimed his authority, which were in fact far removed from His character of love and respect, and nothing to do with Him. I also have to own up that I was as guilty of this as the community at times. God gets blamed for an awful lot of things!

The God of the institutional Church seemed a very rigid unyielding, inflexible kind of Godhead who didn't somehow fit with the loving, compassionate, intensely personal God that I held intimate conversations with. I found orthodox praying increasingly difficult, to the point where it became impossible and phoney. Dom John Chapman was very wise in his adage, 'Pray as you can and not as you can't.'[8] My praying was much more of a conversational dialogue which didn't fit into the composed prayers that corporate praying can sometimes descend into, more the wordless kind of dialogue which didn't need (or want) to be formalised. Words of John Bunyan come to mind: 'When thou prayest, rather let thy heart be without words, than thy words without heart.'[9] Quaint language that holds a wealth of wisdom. Praying with others, despite its important place within the corporate life of the Church, felt increasingly irksome for me, and was a hindrance rather than a help. Prayer for me is intensely personal and private. That way there can be a searing honesty about how I feel which, in the presence of others, I am unable to be. I daresay others echo my sentiments. I identified very much with the kind of concepts Gerard Hughes describes when writing of a particular experience:

> I entered the cathedral to pray but could not at first – at least, not the Lord save me from blisters, sunstroke, motorists type of prayer. I sat and let the vastness of the cathedral and the lines of its arches engender an inner silence and do the praying for me, the kind of praying I had experienced on the island. Not so much an activity I engaged in, as something which engaged me when I was still.[10]

The dilemma for me came when I reached the point of being unable to go along with 'corporate Christianity', for want of a better expression. What was meant to be good news in the rather legalistic and rigid interpretation that was often offered as gospel felt to me to be a distortion of the gospel, and whatever it might have meant for someone else, it did not connect emotionally with me or for me. I had to embark on a process of digesting what I heard and read, seeing and experiencing what it meant to me, at this point in my life. In other words, I had to make it my own, which had profound implications and repercussions. Truly, if the gospel cannot meet us where we are and have something relevant to say, then it has become an empty wineskin, and it may be that we have to discard the old wineskin and allow the Holy Spirit to bring a fresh interpretation, which will need a rather more flexible wineskin to contain it. God is not in a hurry, even if we often are! Resurrection, I am discovering, is an ongoing experience, not a once-and-for all event. As Kahl Rahner once said, 'God is always greater than what we know of him.'[11] When we embrace the idea that God breaks through convention and repeatedly takes the waiting world by surprise, we will perhaps be less surprised when we return to the places where we thought we would find Him and discover, as certain women found on that first resurrection morning, that 'He is not here... He has gone before you into Galilee'.[12] The question was also asked of them, 'Why are you looking among the dead for one who is alive?' Salutary words which I imagine can have relevance for us all when we want to keep God entombed. Never will I forget an experience of sitting in a particular sanctuary on one occasion, feeling very deadened by the prevailing atmosphere, to hear from within me those very words. I found them shocking, particularly given the context in which I heard them. It seemed God himself was prompting me to ask searching questions.

At times like this it can be comforting to recall that the divine angel followed that up by reminding them (and us) that 'He has gone before you.' However dangerous traversing this new territory might feel, we follow in the footsteps of one who was not afraid to ask searching questions or confront religious authorities. Living on the boundary as Jesus did inevitably means risks and challenge, and quite possibly isolation too at times. The enquiring mind rarely has the luxury of comfortable contentment, because there are always new horizons that beckon, which make new demands of us and stretch our comfort zones. Growth is of necessity demanding of personal resources.

I felt a pressure to fit in with the prevailing teaching and outlook and found, as my own understanding and experience of God changed and developed, that I could no longer fit in. I felt myself to be experiencing new wine which was bursting my own limited wineskin. Difficult enough to handle for myself, never mind feeling I was a threat to the institutional Church, to which at that time I belonged. I felt huge pressure to comply with the status quo as it always had been, and whilst I recognise a large part of this was a projection of the huge pressure from within me to remain the same, there was also a substantial degree of reality. The external reality resonated most acutely on my own internal reality.

While so much change and reappraisal was going on within me I could no longer comfortably manage being part of a community that in a sense was unwittingly and constantly pulling me back into the old way of being. The conflict it generated was intolerable and ultimately I decided to leave the Church. This was a decision that affected me more than I had bargained for. Neville Symington, priest and psychoanalyst, made an interesting observation. He writes:

> Many of the most creative minds have had to break free of the stranglehold of the official academies of which they were members... It is a common experience that as a person uncovers a new aspect of himself in an analysis, he will want to study a new book or attend a course of lectures that had not previously held his interest. The instigator of this new flowering of intellectual interest is an inner emotional yearning – the analysis has caused a new emotional reality to exist within the psychological structure.
>
> I believe that to come upon this new inner reality is frightening because it carries with it responsibility. Its possessor must declare ownership of it and this is resisted. Why? Because it means a separation from those with whom the possessor hitherto shared a corporate sense of togetherness. He is on his own. This is such a frightening experience that he is tempted to cover it over and rush back and seek the comfort of warm togetherness.
>
> To live by the guidance of the inner light is terrifying... It can mean forsaking the support of those warm, supportive figures in their outer environment and even more so those in their inner environment. Frequently a patient will cling tenaciously to the

> most tyrannical inner figure rather than face isolated inner loneliness. The patient takes flight in conventionality. He feels comfortable again, supported and no longer lonely. But he has lost a precious treasure that could have been the seed of something true, something genuine, something creative: 'To hide under the cloak of another is a great temptation to human beings, but it spells psychic death.'[13]

Leaving the Church, an organisation to which I had been connected all my life, was a trauma which plunged me into bereavement of colossal proportions. I had frequently to remind myself that 'taking leave of the Church does not necessarily have to mean taking leave of God,' as Philip Richter and Leslie Francis point out in their book about why people leave the Church.[14]

One of the people they interviewed had said, 'I see God and Church as quite distinct.' At that time in my life the two were unhelpfully linked as one, and it took several years before I could comfortably accept that differentiation at an emotional level, even if I agreed wholeheartedly with it at an intellectual level.

Having been born of missionary parents in India, and having myself been a missionary for many years in Africa, it was as if the Church had formed me, and certainly at a psychological level it had. My mandate for missionary service had never been with the aim of proselytising – I have a deeply ingrained loathing of anything that even hints of persuading someone (however nicely packaged and presented) into beliefs that they are either not ready for, or do not want as their own. That approach feels manipulative and seemed particularly hard on vulnerable people who maybe craved acceptance and found it difficult to say no. I now realise this antipathy was born out of my own experience, whereby a succession of Christian schools from my earliest years influenced my thinking with Christian teaching and values, some of which had a distinctly fundamentalist flavour. Such a realisation at the time was deeply unconscious. I only knew freedom for people to follow their heart was immensely important to me – and still is. It is no coincidence that my work now as a therapist is about facilitating and supporting others in the costly business of discovering for themselves what they think and what they believe and the path they wish to walk, which is their own, rather than what others have decided for them, however well-meaning such actions might have been. It's very much a case of 'When I was a child, I thought as a child, but now that I am a man I put away childish things,' as the apostle Paul described this maturing process so eloquently in his letter to the Corinthians.[15]

I discovered there comes a time for all of us, if we want to be ourselves rather than prisoners of our past, when we have to re-evaluate the diet we were brought up on – however tasty or otherwise the morsels were at the time – in order that we choose a diet that is nourishing for us in the here and now. There may well be elements that we keep, but that is because they are worth keeping and because we have chosen to, which is very different to swallowing wholesale what others decide for us. It is about developing the capacity to make choices, and even more about the ability to be able to say 'no thanks, that's not for me' without the crippling guilt that tries to sabotage independence, or the apologetic need to justify one's particular tastes, as if somehow there was not room for diversity in the spiritual diet. But then, as is well-known, the fundamentalist position about anything is in itself a desperate strategy to prevent unconscious doubt from becoming conscious, making different opinions very threatening. And the more frightening the possibility that one's well-held views might not be as water-tight as we were led to believe, the greater the pressure to accept wholesale what you are told as 'gospel'. It will not be difficult for the imaginative reader to realise how threatening my questioning and enquiring mind was both to myself and to the church community, particularly as my questions would not be silenced through anything other than the authentic discoveries I made for myself.

I found myself having insights and experiences that felt like discovering the 'pearl of great price' to which Jesus likened the Kingdom of Heaven. But of course in order to find, and more importantly recognise, something so precious and worthwhile requires a great deal of searching, which is time-consuming and all absorbing. It is a process that for me evolves gradually, alongside a willingness to relinquish other 'pearls' which no longer satisfy, even if at earlier stages they were both enjoyable and satisfying. The Merchant Trader of the parable traded what he had for what he wanted, and the currency he used had necessarily built up over many years experience in trading in pearls. As a result he was able to recognise the real thing when he saw it, and even more, I imagine, when he held it for himself. It is only when we have held something ourselves that we can know intuitively whether this new discovery, this new experience feels right for us. Having found the real thing, the thing for which he had been searching, the merchant trader was willing and ready to part with what he had, in order to afford this most precious pearl. HA Williams, in his commentary on this parable makes an interesting observation. He writes:

> Jesus said that the Kingdom of Heaven was like this merchant man. At the very least this means that the Kingdom is not something which can be immediately presented to you on a plate, so that all you have to do is to put it into your pocket and feel good. You will find many devout Christians who have forgotten what Jesus said and who will present the kingdom of heaven to you in exactly this way. It means they will tell you, adhesion to a given form of doctrinal orthodoxy. Believe this, that and the other, and there, you've got the kingdom. But you haven't got it. All you've got is an excuse to stop looking for it.
>
> Or, some people will tell you that the kingdom consists of obedience to a traditional system of ethics. Do this and don't do that, and yours is the kingdom. Obedience of this kind often looks like a virtue. In fact it is always a blasphemy. A blasphemy against oneself. To base and regulate one's life upon other people's rules – even when they call them God's law – this is blasphemous because it is to choose slavery when you could be free. Freedom involves the discovery by each of us of the law of his own being, 'how he, as a unique person' can express sincerely and fearlessly what he is.[16]

Strong language that cuts through respectability and makes an impact – not unlike the manner and teaching of Jesus, which as I recall, on occasions shocked the religious authorities of His day and got him into all sorts of trouble. Growth implies change and movement. And for that to happen we have to be prepared to let go of the familiar for something new. In a very real sense, loss and gain are very much tied up with one another, and sometimes it can be our fear of losing what we have that holds us back from grasping with both hands what we could have. Without a doubt risk is involved, and trust, which are big issues for many, if not all of us. The psychoanalyst Margaret Arden talks of 'the healing process as a natural tendency. The essential requirement for healing to occur is the establishment of trust'.[17]

Trust in the healing process, trust in that healing capacity within ourselves, and trust in God as representative of that which is other and greater than ourselves.

Trust was certainly an issue which the Israelites of old struggled with on their epic journey from slavery into freedom. I don't wonder they made such a successful film out of the Exodus story, because at a symbolic level we can all identify with the quest to move on from our own unique versions of Egypt to what constitutes our 'promised land'. The story grips us precisely because experientially we know what a struggle it can be to trust, especially at those moments when it feels as if we are being asked to take huge risks in the name of personal growth and greater freedom, with no guarantees that at the end we will find what we are wanting. For the Israelites it revealed itself time and again in the pull to go back to the oppression they knew in Egypt as soon as there was any hint of difficulty, rather than the sustained resolve to move forward to their promised land with all that that implies, of setbacks to be overcome rather than having an easy ride; a concept Symington spoke of in the excerpt quoted above. The known, even if it is terrible, is familiar. To move into the unknown requires courage and an ability and willingness to take risks. George Eliot in *Middlemarch* wrote 'Upon my word, I think the truth is the hardest missile one can be pelted with.'

However, I was yet to discover that embarking on this journey is no easy task. It wasn't for the Children of Israel way back in the days of the Egyptian Pharaohs when they felt oppressed and in bondage to controlling others whose clarion call was to demand more, more, more. No matter how many bricks were produced it was never enough as the Biblical account in Exodus, chapter five makes clear. Not surprisingly, such relentless pressure was unsustainable and eventually broke their spirit, which is what happens now when any of us are enslaved to cruel dictators, either literally, in the form of those who demand more and more of us, or from within ourselves in the form of the internal figures that all of us have, which shape the way we think and behave and can pressurise us in unhelpful ways. For example, that familiar pressure when we sit down to relax and a multitude of things to be done suddenly take on an unhelpful urgency that, if we don't stand up to and resist, has us running round in an endless cycle of activity.

As has already been demonstrated, the external bully figures that pressurise us and give us a hard time only do so because they find a ready resonance and vulnerability in that element within ourselves. We have to learn how to set limits on the demands from within us before there can be any hope of standing up to the pressures generated from external sources. This realisation can be very salutary as we begin to assimilate the ways we ourselves have contributed to our own suffering. Most of us, I suspect, like to preserve the fantasy that our difficulties and struggles are all down to others! However much that may have been an initial factor, it is we ourselves who have unwittingly perpetuated the unhappiness in the way we relate to ourselves and others. Locating the source of all our troubles 'out there' undoubtedly makes for a more comfortable, easier life initially, but sells us short of meaningful and satisfying relationships. We discover that unhelpful patterns of relating have a nasty habit of repeating themselves until finally we get the message and realise such repetitions are a call from within ourselves to understand and resolve, in order that something new can take its place. Hopefully something that is more satisfying and meaningful and contributes to the enjoyment of life rather than just getting by. Margaret Arden adds to this debate when she writes:

> Another basic Christian idea which is important to me as an analyst is that Jesus said, 'Unless you become like little children, you shall not enter the kingdom of heaven.' This is my marker of the true self. False self behaviour is usually manipulative and destructive of psychic truth. All our theories can be seen as ways of unravelling the destructive processes or defences which the patient uses. The miracle of psychoanalysis – and it is a miracle – is that when a person comes to understand the core of his or her

> childhood experience, all the anger, all the rejection of life, turns out to have been for one purpose – to preserve, at whatever cost, the child who is capable of love.[18]

The journey into greater personal freedom, literal and symbolic, is about discovering our true selves and allowing the spontaneous, loving child we all once were to increasingly be rediscovered and set free to live, rather than eking out an existence of sorts with significant parts of ourselves hidden away. Such a journey must of necessity take time because by its very nature it is one of discovery, which will include oases as well as setbacks, and at times even what appear to be insurmountable obstacles to overcome. I imagine arriving at the Red Sea was such a moment for the Israelites, yet significantly a way did open up for them, so that the seemingly impossible became possible. History tells us they took forty years to reach their Promised Land, which is another way of saying a very long time! Even a quick reading of the Exodus account of that journey reveals how demanding of personal resources it was – and continues to be in the particular journeys we embark upon. It also highlights the pull to return to Egypt as soon as the going got tough, which I daresay most of us can identify with. When personal growth stretches our familiar boundaries and the going gets tough, there is that part in all of us that whispers enticingly to encourage us back into old and familiar ways of being. It never ceases to amaze me how strong is the pull to remain in pain, rather than move on to the metaphorical Promised Land which is a calling for all of us.

It can be very tempting to pray for a miracle that will rescue us from whatever is our particular trial, which could therefore serve as a short cut and save us the sheer hard work that healing in its widest context entails. There have been churches that have encouraged this kind of thinking and caused further suffering in the process when healing hasn't happened in the way the disappointed believer hoped. Happily, this sort of thing happens less and less, but still happens as I can testify to both personally and through people who I have been alongside in their sense of failure when the prayer for healing hasn't happened, or not in the way that was expected and hoped. Healing, by its very nature is a process of growth and regeneration, upon which cause and effect have an influence. Witness our bodies which, even from a simple cut or graze, require time to heal and come together again, and this process is magnified following major surgery. If that is so for physical healing how much more so is it for emotional wounds, many of which have the magnitude of major surgery in their impact on our minds and souls? It seems understanding and compassion can be extended for physical wounds but not so often for their emotional counterparts which are no less difficult and traumatic to come to terms with and heal. Often they are more so as they are hidden beneath the coping exterior that has to get on with life, in spite of traumas which, if they were visible, would invite compassion and concern. Margaret Arden in her thoughts on the healing process has this to say:

> If we think about mental processes as analogous to physical processes, we can suppose that there is a natural healing tendency in the mind which corresponds to the healing of physical wounds. The separation of mind and body is an idea which is no longer tenable.
>
> The process of healing can be brought about by other kinds of relationships than psychotherapy, and also by significant experiences, including religious ones. I think the capacity for such experiences is closely connected with creativity, whatever that is. In any event we are looking at the replacement of abnormal mental patterns by healthy ones.[19]

We are what we think, and changing how we think is hugely significant. I have always loved the Biblical character Moses, with his difficulty in believing in himself arising out of a difficult beginning in life. How could he not struggle with his identity and a haunting sense of not really belonging, when for the best of reasons his own mother had to abandon him to a basket in the river? Traumatic for her, but doubly so for the infant Moses, who at that stage in his life would have no understanding of why he was so suddenly and traumatically separated from his mother. He was brought up in a palace by his sister, who had to pretend she wasn't, and a queen who liked the idea of having a baby but wasn't, as far as we know, particularly interested in being with him, enjoying his developing personality and investing time in getting to know him. I'm sure it was no coincidence that his calling by God to lead the Israelites out of their bondage in Egypt was also the story that underlay my vocation to Africa. We both had issues to deal with and this was to start the process of leading me out of my particular bondage, quite apart from anything I might do for anyone else. The two are usually linked, as it was for Moses whose personal growth was challenged every bit as much as the people he was leading. Of course he doubted his ability to take on such a challenge. Up until that point he had had to hide his potential and his true identity, so I imagine such a calling to literally come up front and be seen was terrifying.

I went to Africa out of a clear sense of vocation, with no particular task in mind, because I felt sure this was where I was meant to be. I wondered what I would do, as 'doing' was all that had hitherto defined me. My husband, as a doctor, had a more specific role, but mine was one which I had to discover. Letter after letter would arrive, asking what I was doing. In fact, I ended up with an ever changing role as family responsibilities changed, which included taking up the role of primary school teacher to our sons until they could go to the nearest English-speaking school, a two-hour flight away in the capital, teaching women to read, using in limited form my nursing and midwifery training within the hospital setting, teaching hygiene in the Bible School to pastors' wives, assisting in the pharmacy, offering hospitality and sewing clothes for family and colleagues, in tandem with my primary vocations as a wife and mother. In a weak moment I offered to make seventy shirts for the nurses' uniforms to silence the pressure I felt (mostly from within me) as a newly-arrived missionary to be doing something that might sound worthy to supporters back home. All the while I was adjusting to a very different lifestyle, with a toddler to care for who was making his own adjustments. An illustration of the concept I was writing about earlier, how primarily it is the pressure within ourselves that drives us to do and achieve inappropriately.

Life in the jungle makes one become very resourceful, and I loved the challenges that a more basic lifestyle without consistent water or electricity presented. Rain was a cause of great excitement, not least because falling rain on our corrugated iron roofs drained along the guttering and into our water tanks. On many an occasion when there was no fuel for the generator to pump water, we would rise in the night to fill our buckets and pour them into the old fuel barrels we kept in the house for use in the bathroom and kitchen.

I recall one Christmas pondering how I could bake a Christmas cake on a single charcoal brazier, which was all we had in the early days before we rose to the heights of luxury in having a wood-burning stove! The solution was for me to lift the tin box oven on and off the charcoal brazier, so that it cooked slowly and without burning. Four hours later the cake was done. Having so successfully negotiated this hurdle, and even acquired icing sugar all the way from the capital, a thousand miles away, I duly put the iced cake in the fridge on Christmas Eve, to keep the ants from feasting on it before we did. On Christmas morning I opened the fridge door to discover that putting a whole cake in was too much for our temperamental kerosene fridge, which had defrosted overnight and dripped onto the iced cake. There was Santa, having slid onto his side, looking half drunk! However, the icing had taken the brunt of the water and the cake beneath was fine and much enjoyed by us all. I also discovered I needed to learn, initially by trial and error, the art of hairdressing for myself, my family and our colleagues. My salon was the very fine front verandah of our house which was built on a huge anthill, and therefore from its elevated position enjoyed magnificent views across the river. The river was a mile wide at this point and served as the most reliable communication system for the country, with dug out canoes laden with market produce propelling themselves close to the banks, and the rather larger barges carrying goods and people from the capital up the thousand miles to where we were. Such were the joys of life in the jungle! A sense of humour was, as ever, essential for survival.

However, Africa's greatest gift to me was to begin to teach me what it was to 'be'. This was new territory and was immensely threatening to someone whose whole basis of value was about what one did, as opposed to simply being oneself. It never occurred to me that the person I was, and developed into, was of far more significance to God than anything I might do and achieve. And so began an inner journey when I began to discover what it meant to be 'led by the Spirit into all truth'.[20] The truth that is, about oneself. Jesus was also led by the Spirit into the wilderness at the very start of his public ministry and we are interestingly told very little about the experiences He had there except that 'angels came and ministered to him.' Having myself begun to experience what it means to be led into the truth about myself, I can well understand his need for angels to minister to him. I'm inclined to agree with George Eliot when he spoke of 'truth as the hardest missile one can be pelted with,' certainly when it comes to 'inside truth' precisely because it touches us at the very core of our being. Anyone embarking on this inner journey will need angels in one form or another to support and encourage them along the way. I have been deeply grateful for particular people who have served in that capacity for me.

One of the things I love about geographical journeys is their capacity to widen horizons and offer a different view of life. In the process of journeying what we see affects us and makes its own impact, which inevitably means we change as people. This will have its effect not only on our thinking processes but will translate into and through our bodies, which express so eloquently in their own way all that is happening to us. Our fatigues and hungers, our aches and pains, are all a language that we need to become familiar with. The inner journey is no different, and our bodies are a valuable form of communication about how we really feel and what we really think. We might say 'I'm fine,' but our bodies may well reflect a very different state of affairs. Brian Broom, a consultant physician and psychotherapist has made this mind/body link the title of his very fine book. He has this to say in an early chapter –

> The focus is on the person as a whole. This person presents to the clinician with symptoms in the body. The bodily symptoms are considered carefully, along with the story of the whole person, and a working hypothesis is developed as to the meaning of the symptoms. The clinician and patient then join in a collaborative journey of discovery and healing.[21]

An exploration into the faces of anger cannot ignore our bodies, which are such an integral part of us and therefore serve as a vehicle of expression, particularly if we are unable to allow particular thoughts and feelings to become conscious in any other way. So, from the context within which my thinking developed, we move to taking a closer look at our bodies.

---

NOTES

[7] Mathew 15:9

[8] Robert Jeffrey; *Anima Christi: Reflections on praying with Christ*, Darton, Longman and Todd, 1994, p.8

[9] John Bunyen, quoted in, *Meditations and prayers for Illumination*, edited by Rowland Croucher, Albatross, 1994

[10] Gerard Hughes, *In Search of a Way*, Darton, Longman and Todd, 1978, p.70

[11] Matthew, Sheila and Dennis Linn, *Healing Religious Addiction*, Darton, Longman and Todd, 1995, p.14

[12] Luke 24:6

[13] Neville Symington, *The Making of a Psychotherapist*, Karnac Books Ltd, 1996, p.16

[14] Philip Richter and Leslie Francis, *Gone but not Forgotten*, Darton Longman and Todd, 1998

[15] 1 Corinthians 13:11

[16] HA Williams, *The True Wilderness*, first published by Constable and Co. Ltd, 1965, pp.51/52

[17] Margaret Arden, *Midwifery of the Soul*, Free Association Books Ltd, 1998, p.97

[18] Margaret Arden, *Midwifery of the Soul*, Free Association Books Ltd, 1998, p5

[19] Margaret Arden, *Midwifery of the Soul*, Free Association Books Ltd, 1998, p.85

[20] John 16:13

[21] Brian Broom, *Somatic Illness: The Patients Other Story*, Free Association Books Ltd, 1997, p.4

## *The Body*

As a prelude to focussing on the faces of anger, it feels important for us to think about our bodies and the significant part they play in determining how we feel by communicating feeling states to us. We are sensate beings and everything that happens to us and that we experience gets registered within our bodies. They are our most important asset, as well as a gift entrusted to us by the Creator, which is ours for the keeping until we die. They are also, as the apostle Paul reminds us, 'temples of the Holy Spirit,'[22] a fact we sometimes lose sight of when we drive ourselves relentlessly and live out punishing schedules. They are the containers within which we move about and communicate, out of which all creative thought emanates. We abuse them at our peril, as subsequent chapters will reveal. Yet unwittingly, for a variety of reasons, all of us have at times a tendency to ignore the signals that indicate there is trouble brewing. We also seem to take for granted the joy of a healthily functioning body, until symptoms appear – and then we're desperate for someone to make it better!

Our bodies give us each our own unique identity that enables others to recognise you as you and me as me. I find it a rather wonderful thought that there is no other human being with my particular identity. The psychoanalyst Judith Hubback writes about this very sense of 'me-ness' with reference to the text quoted earlier from 1 Corinthians 6, using the old authorised version of the Bible.

> Some people find the idea of God helps them to be sure they have their own me-ness and to know that every other individual also has that. For example, one of the earliest Christians, St Paul, wrote 'Know ye not that your body is the temple of the Holy Ghost, which is in you, which ye have of God, and ye are not your own.' (1 Corinthians 6:19). That is an assertion of the belief that something very remarkable – Holy Ghost, spirit or self – lives in the body. Other people do not like bringing any god into

the matter; they find the boundary of human dimension suits them better than the difficult combination of boundlessness and comprehensiveness that there is in the deity.[23]

Of course, having a body immediately presupposes that all important boundary between where I end and you begin, between what the eminent paediatrician and psychoanalyst DW Winnicott referred to as 'me versus not-me'. Learning to differentiate ourselves from others is, in varying degrees, the lifelong task for us all, along with containing and being able to contain, the feelings and experiences, thoughts and fantasies that go to make each of us the people we are. When this containing function breaks down, or has never really developed because of difficulties in the early mother-baby relationship, the skin may be the vehicle that conveys a difficulty in this area, for example when rashes, eczema or psoriasis break out, though I hasten to add it is never quite as simple as that as Brian Broom points out in a section from his book entitled *The Language of the Body*. He writes:

> The holistic task is very difficult. Reducing the person to that which is currently measurable is untenable, but is it really possible to get very far by in-depth study of an individual with whom the clinician is in relationship? Joyce McDougall, a psychoanalyst, provides a stimulating contribution to this question in her book *Theatres of the Body* (1989), in which she discusses the psychotherapy of physical illness.
> 
> A major emphasis is on the concept of disease or illness as language. For most clinicians such a concept is preposterous, but in working with such somatisers over the years I have gradually come to see that in a patients choice of disorder it is often possible to discern a statement, or a language of the body. Illness (or some illnesses) seen from this perspective is construed as a form of communication.
> 
> A sixty-year-old woman came with a florid facial rash, of five years standing, resistant to all previous treatments. She had even had her liver biopsied on suspicion of a carcinoid tumour. She was referred for an allergy opinion but I could find no evidence of allergic factors. But in response to my question, 'What has been the most difficult thing in your life over the last six years?' she promptly replied: 'My husband's illness.' I then asked her how it had affected her, and she said: 'Oh, I keep a brave face on

> it.' Noting her choice of words I asked her the same question five minutes later, and again she used the same wording. I drew her attention to the possible linkage between her facial rash and the 'brave face'. A week later I spent a further hour providing a cathartic opportunity for her bottled up feelings, and within ten days from first assessment her rash had gone.
>
> This rash appears to have been a statement, in the soma, of things unable to be expressed in verbal language. It is a moot point whether her healing was due to putting the feelings in verbal language, or whether it was due to the fact that at last she was heard.[24]

We are unique and complex beings and, as Joyce McDougall points out in her paper "In every case the symptom tells a story... There is little doubt that every psychological event has its effect upon the physiological body, just as every somatic event has repercussions on the mind, even if these are not consciously registered. Industrial research has produced convincing statistics to demonstrate that people are more apt to fall ill, need operations or have accidents when they are feeling depressed or anxious than when they feel fulfilled or optimistic about their lives."[25]

Our skin serves as that all important literal boundary, holding our muscles, bones and bodily organs inside, providing a barrier that helps protect us from harmful external stimuli. It is not surprising that such an acutely sensitive and intuitively perceptive substance serves as a carrier for our feeling states. The way we were held and nurtured as infants mattered then and matters still, forming a prototype upon which all other experiences in that field get superimposed. Feelings are the body's radar system, keeping us informed about how we're doing. Signals are being transmitted and received all the time. What a tragedy when feelings, that most precious gift, are stifled and ignored. Our bodies at times cry out our distress in physical pain of one sort or another, that is a symptom of our unease but alas, so often those signals from our soul are ignored, and silenced through drugs, alcohol, being busy and turning a deaf ear, to name but a few. Joyce McDougall in her paper, given to a symposium in Paris in 1974 on the psychoanalytic process, made this comment about this ability to ignore pain:

Allied to the physiological 'hardiness' of many a psychosomatic patient is a character trait which is a frequent manifestation in psychosomatic personalities: the refusal to give in to psychic pain, anguish or depression. This gives an impression of superhuman emotional control... The lines of a modern folk song by Simon and Garfunkel epitomise this character trait:

> 'I touch no one
> And no one touches me.
> I am a rock,
> I am an island
> And a rock feels no pain
> And an island never cries.

The baby who cannot create within himself his mothers' image to deal with his pain is a lonely island. One way out is to turn oneself into a rock.[26]

It is important to stress that there are reasons why any of us choose to behave and act in particular ways. This way of being serves a particular purpose in our psychic economy, protecting us from re-experiencing intolerable pain that we know about unconsciously even if for the time being it has not surfaced into conscious awareness. The body will know, and very often indicates its inner knowing by nameless anxieties that begin to surface if we don't defend against them. This seems to have been a factor in what drove a particular patient for analysis. I quote from a paper given by the psychoanalyst Elliott Jaques. He writes:

> Mr N had led a successful life by everyday standards up to the time he came into analysis. He was an active man, a doer. He had been successful in his career through intelligent application and hard work, was married with children and many good friends, and all seemed to be going very well.
>
> The idealised content of this picture had been maintained by an active carrying on of life without allowing time for reflection. His view was that he had not come to analysis for himself, but rather for a kind of tutorial purpose – he would bring his case history to me and we would have a clinical seminar in which we would conduct a psychoanalytic evaluation of the case material he presented.
>
> As might be expected, Mr N had great difficulty in coping with ambivalence. He was unconsciously frightened of any

> resentment, envy, jealousy or any other hostile feeling towards me, maintaining an attitude of idealised love for me and tolerant good nature towards every attempt on my part to analyse the impulses of destructiveness and the feelings of persecution which he was counteracting by this idealisation.
>
> When we finally did break through this inability to cope with ambivalence, it emerged that in all his relationships his idealisation was inevitably followed by disappointment – a disappointment arising out of failure to get the quality of love he was expecting, and nursed by the envy of those whom he idealised.
>
> He admitted he was ill, and that unconscious awareness of his illness undoubtedly was the main reason for his seeking analysis. Being active and over concerned for others were soporifics to which he had become addicted. Indeed, he confessed he had resented my analysis taking this defensive addiction away from him. He had secretly entertained ideas of stopping his analysis 'because all this thinking about myself, instead of doing things, is no good. Now I realise that I have been piling up my rage against you inside myself, like I've done with everyone else.'[27]

The author's comment on his patient's busyness 'without allowing time for reflection' reminds me of a remark Nelson Mandela made on the BBC television programme *Breakfast with Frost*. They were reflecting together upon his long prison experience and his current role as president of the ANC. Nelson Mandela made the poignant remark that what he missed most about life in prison was the time it gave him for reflection. He commented upon his current lifestyle, which was filled with people and events from early morning until very late at night, and satisfying and meaningful as that was he added, 'I have no proper time to think', and cautioned others as well as himself on the dangers of being in this position.

Picking up on another theme from Elliott Jaques, the comment 'being active and over concerned for others were soporifics to which he had become addicted', a phrase which may well find a resonance within all of us from time to time, as any addiction can be incredibly painful to relinquish. It has to be understood that it serves a particular purpose for us in warding off feelings that for very legitimate internal reasons we are afraid of.

The authors of *Healing Religious Addiction* write, 'I've learned that an addiction is any substance or process we use to escape from and get control over a painful reality in our lives, especially painful feelings. We use something outside to escape from and control something we're afraid of inside.'[28]

To attend to our pain takes time and effort. It also takes a great deal of courage. It causes us to re-evaluate life and make changes as we begin to discover what is healthy and what is not. Do we want life and all that could lead us to growth and development and more fulfilment and satisfaction in living, or do we prefer death and all that in one form or another is destructive to that inner life-giving process, killing off emotional vitality and therefore life? Of course at a conscious level we don't on the whole choose death, yet unconsciously it seems other forces are at work within us that can sabotage all that goes to bring us to life, by which I mean all that contributes to feeling gloriously alive as we increasingly realise our potential and fulfil ourselves in the fullest possible way.

The choice is ours, though rarely is it as simple as that. In a very real sense every day we are making choices by the things we do and say which have consequences and repercussions. The problem comes, as Elliot Jacques makes clear in his paper quoted earlier, when we act without giving ourselves enough space to reflect on the direction in which our lives are heading. We end up reacting rather than responding. We can sometimes see with greater clarity other people who might be on a course of self-destruction, as we glibly say, without necessarily applying such observations to ourselves – because of course it's much more comfortable to distance ourselves from such uncomfortable realities. The parable about noticing and being more concerned with the speck in our brother's eye whilst ignoring the plank in our own might have timely meaning for all of us![29]

One path is more likely to lead to life and growth, fulfilment and joy. It will also embrace pain as a part of what it means to feel fully alive. The other leads ultimately to emotional deadness, for the dead, like the rock of Simon and Garfunkel's song, cannot feel, and one of the functions of our particular addiction is that it should silence the pain of feelings. Sadly this can, and most probably will, ultimately lead to being physically alive but emotionally deadened and therefore in that sense having no life. The consequence of this state of affairs is to leave a person emotionally hungry and driven to unconsciously feed off the vitality of others in a parasitic kind of way. Tragically when any of us kill off important aspects of ourselves, we can become both deadened and deadening. By this I mean that within that kind of situation it can be exceedingly difficult to maintain one's own vitality and life. After a period of time in the company of such people, you can feel drained and deeply tired, depleted by them of your psychic vitality. An example of this kind of experience comes to mind from David Furlong, writing in his book *The Healer Within*. He writes:

> The story of a well-known healer who was also a vicar adds a further dimension to this form of experience. One particular patient used to visit the vicar on a regular basis and seemed to gain much help from the contact, until one day he missed his appointment. For many months he never got back in touch, but in the mean time the healer, for no apparent reason and at all sorts of odd times, would suddenly feel totally drained of energy. He could not understand what was happening and thought he must have some form of illness. Eventually the healer accidentally bumped into his patient again and asking how he fared, was met with a very sheepish expression. The patient confessed that he had been sorry to have missed the appointment, which was caused by some unforeseen circumstances. Feeling so desperate for healing he confessed to having 'tuned into' the healer and had then felt an immediate beneficial response. The patient then concluded from this that perhaps it was not necessary to actually see the particular healer as he was a busy person. Instead, whenever he needed help he just 'tuned in' and felt healing energy coming to him from the healer. The vicar felt the penny drop as he realised why he had suddenly felt so tired at all sorts of different times.[30]

Whatever you may feel about that incident and the issues it raises about personal boundaries, it illustrates that we are all giving off emotional signals, and that contact with others has its emotional impact. The gospel story of the healing of the woman with a longstanding haemorrhage also illustrates this concept. We are told she touched the hem of Jesus' garment and 'experienced a healing within her'. The point I am making in this context is the response of Jesus to this incident, when amidst a large crowd of jostling people he says, 'Someone touched me for I knew it when power went out of me.'[31]

The path that leads to death in the sense of which we are speaking, avoids much conscious pain, avoids conflict, avoids thinking. It's a path that says 'here, eat this, it will do you good' as Eve did in the ancient Garden of Eden, persuading Adam to eat the fruit with disastrous consequences. Ultimately we realise we have been sold a lie and what was sold as good in fact feels anything but good. That is the trouble with accepting what others tell you. We have to find out for ourselves on a taste and see basis.

Our bodies have a way of speaking their truth, and it is our task to each learn the language of our bodies – which, I might add, will be unique to each of us. Let me illustrate this with an excerpt from Joyce McDougall's paper:

> A patient reported a war experience in which a bomb exploded beside him, killing his companions while he was knocked unconscious. He recovered unhurt except that his skin was covered with great patches of psoriasis, an affliction until then unknown to him. We cannot say that the explosion caused the outbreak: it overthrew his usual psychic defences in the face of danger, laying him open to somatic explosion. No doubt everyone has a threshold beyond which his psychic defence work can no longer cope, at which moment the body bears the brunt.[32]

Very often it is colloquial language that we find ourselves using which offers a clue in understanding what our bodies may be trying to communicate through various metaphors. Here are a few that immediately come to mind: Stiff upper lip. You get up my nose. Get off my back. A pain in the neck. Two-faced. You get under my skin. Hold your tongue. He was the apple of my eye. Broken-hearted. Get it off your chest. It makes me sick. Can't stomach it. The permutations and possibilities are endless. We need to listen to these communications from our inner selves and find out what exactly makes us sick, rather than just going back for more until our bodies express their protest even louder, either through illness or total breakdown, so that we are forced to take notice. Repairing a car that has broken down is a rather more costly and time-consuming procedure than attending to it when the warning light comes on to indicate there is a problem somewhere in the system. I recall on one occasion ignoring the red oil light, thinking, regrettably, that it could wait until later. Alas, the engine expressed its protest noisily to the point of almost grinding to a halt as I just made it to a garage. I ended up with a hefty garage bill and a lot of inconvenience, which could have been remedied so much easier if I had more fully understood the significance of the warning light in that context, and begun to attend to it at the time, rather than feeling it could wait. I learnt a salutary lesson that day. It also very nearly cost me my car.

Paradoxically, to choose life is to sign up to pain and to feelings, because becoming increasingly alive has necessarily to mean that we will increasingly feel, and if you come alive to your feelings, you open the door to feeling everything. Not all at once of course, that would be too much and do damage, but as and when they arise. Of course it is opening the door to feelings that can be so frightening, causing us at times to choose the path that kills off life – unconsciously that is. This happens every time decisions based on gaining approval from others are made, rather than following our hearts and being true to what feels right for us. This path will inevitably set up all sorts of conflicts if what we want is different to what the prevailing group around us thinks, be that family, friends, work colleagues or whoever. Then we begin to realise how deep is the longing for approval. For most of us there is layer upon layer of it, which of necessity takes time and a good deal of effort to understand and begin to overcome.

To dare to be one's own person, to take that risk in saying what we think, rather than what we think is possibly expected of us – if not from our actual external world, almost certainly from the people who control us from within ourselves, is very difficult. Our internal worlds that are formed from all the experiences that have gone into shaping each one of us into the people we currently are. It is the making of a community out of the many disparate forces within ourselves that is the lifelong task for all of us, so that there is a place for each within us. Martin Smith comments that 'the range of human experience which we see on a grand scale in society and the world is present in miniature, so to speak, within ourselves. My self is not merely the personality I cultivate for public presentation. There are a host of other selves which just as truly belong to the whole of me.'[33]

In practice this means that certain elements no longer have to protest so loudly in order to be heard, while other elements that have long been banished as either far too dangerous, or not valued for the contribution they make to our total functioning, begin to feel accepted. Equally, the particularly vociferous aspects of ourselves which maybe have tended to rule the roost, may have to learn to accept they are only part of our total structure. This can only have positive repercussions in terms of our total well-being, because instead of being a city divided within itself, we shall be increasingly in harmony and therefore more able to live harmoniously with ourselves and the world around us. Living in the centre of a civil war can only magnify our stress! We will also have so many more resources available within ourselves out of which to live life. The Gospel story of Legion illustrates what can happen when we haven't been able to integrate the many different elements of our personality into a more accepting and acceptable whole. The poor man was tormented by the conflict within himself. He was also very insightful. On being asked his name he replied, 'Legion – for we are many'. Sister Margaret Magdalen CSMV gives a helpful commentary on this story. She writes:

> Whatever the cause of the conflict within him – whether we view it as mental or physical illness, personality or behavioural rather than organic or demonic possession – temporarily it gave him an exceptional strength that he was turning on himself in terrible self-destruction. So violent was he that no one could constrain him, control him or safely get close enough to help him. Thus he continues relentlessly to tear and gash himself, snapping chains like twigs and ripping his clothes in pieces.[34]

The story illustrates something of the self-destructiveness that I was mentioning earlier, and highlights so well the dilemma of healing which we both want but are afraid of in terms of the demands that changing from sabotaging ourselves to choosing the path that leads to life will demand of us. As Margaret Magdalen points out, 'The healing of Legion is the healing we all need in varying degrees.'

It will very soon be discovered that certain of our internal members make more noise than others, while others that have been banished altogether as being much too frightening can be reintegrated back into our living space. Anger is one of these that is either dismissed altogether, with a great deal of energy used in ensuring it never makes an appearance, or it is tolerated but seen as shameful and treated more like a pariah, an outcast. Our task is to value the different elements of ourselves, harness the resources they bring and allow them to contribute creatively to all that makes us individually us. Using up energy to keep certain emotions banished from our conscious awareness can leave us as individuals depleted and tired. Never let it be forgotten that anger is pure energy. What we do with it is up to each of us. The energy is there for us to harness. Burying it is to deprive ourselves of a great deal of energy that could go into living life.

Coming to life emotionally is not unlike the pain of frozen extremities as they thaw out – it hurts, but it's necessary if life is to be re-found and preserved. And within all of us is the continual conflict between the path that leads to life, and the path that leads to death. We all have experiences of things that bring us to life and make us feel joyously, vibrantly alive, and equally, I'm sure we all have experience of situations that deaden us, that leave us feeling heavy, that for one reason or another kill off vitality. Sometimes it can be as simple as having made the wrong decision, when perhaps the decision has been influenced by what others think rather than what we really think, and our bodies with that wilting sensation, are conveying to us that an unhealthy decision has been made.

Within all of us are various instincts, as I have mentioned, and depending upon the events that have shaped and moulded us these instincts, like the currents of the sea, are always there, pulling us this way and that, and the conscious part of ourselves is what helps recognise and direct these instincts so that they work for us rather than against us. I earlier referred to this pull towards that which kills off life as the 'death instinct', by which I mean the part within us that wants to kill off anything life-giving or growth-promoting. The part of us that says 'you'll never manage, so you might as well give up now', the part that says 'you can't', the bit that holds us back, that causes us to doubt ourselves, the bit that is overly cautious, that whispers 'do be careful... are you sure you will manage?', the bit that is always hovering in the wings with dire warnings and threats of reprisals if we dare to challenge, take risks and come to our own conclusions. In other words, if we dare to think differently and independently. It is to that destructive voice, that operates to some degree within all of us, that we need to say, as Jesus once did to someone getting in the way of him achieving His purpose, 'Get behind me Satan'. It amuses me that Jesus is sometimes portrayed as this gentle, endlessly patient person who never lost his rag, yet we have several instances of him coming out with the most outrageous statements! He knew how to make his point in an assertive way that left no-one in any doubt as to what he felt. Not insignificantly, it was one of his closest disciples to whom he had to address this firm rebuke. Significantly this encounter with anger did not destroy their relationship, but on the contrary deepened it.

Very often it is our closest relatives and companions who, for one reason or another, have a personal investment in holding us back, keeping us 'small', keeping us from fulfilling our destiny, because the whole idea of change is anxiety-provoking and threatening. Inevitably when we change it arouses feelings in others which can be difficult to manage if the whole idea of change is frightening and unsettling. After all, who knows where it will lead when once the status quo is challenged and questioned? Dr M Scott Peck, elaborating on the impact of change, particularly as our own map of reality needs updating, writes:

> There come many points on one's journey of spiritual growth whether one is alone or has a psychotherapist as guide, when one must take new and unfamiliar actions in consonance with one's new world view. The taking of such new action – behaving differently from the way one has always behaved before – may represent an extraordinary personal risk.[35]

Freud is much maligned in some circles but has much to teach us about the mind, and had this to say in a paper he wrote on the unconscious: 'It is a very remarkable thing that the unconscious of one human being can react upon that of another without passing through the conscious.'[36] This is why, without even a word being said, we pick up changes in others that can be deeply threatening if they touch an area of ourselves with which we are not yet comfortable. Feeling threatened could be seen as a call to further growth, which necessarily involves pain, much as most of us hanker for growth without pain.

The destructive element that wants to sabotage our development by holding us back in various ways is the part we all struggle with in varying degrees. Its function is to keep us from following our destiny and becoming who we have it in us to be. Mostly, it comes from within us, and sometimes, as with Jesus, it comes through the voices of our nearest and dearest, although he had his share of inner struggle in the wilderness and in Gethsemane. The point is that the remarks of others would hold less power if they didn't so easily find a resonance inside us. That's where the real damage gets done, however much we might like to blame others, our circumstances, or the world.

If we choose life, then we have to take full responsibility for ourselves – and that can be easier said than done. Neville Symington makes a helpful comment on this when he says:

> I believe that to come upon this new inner reality is frightening because it carries with it responsibility. Its possessor must declare ownership of it, and this is resisted – why? Because it means a separation from those with whom the possessor hitherto shared a corporate sense of togetherness. He is on his own. This is such a frightening experience that he is tempted to cover it over and rush back and seek the cover of warm togetherness.
>
> To hide under the cloak of another is a great temptation but it spells psychic death.[37]

Blaming others is a sure sign that we are abdicating responsibility, and blaming never helped anyone, least of all ourselves. It keeps us trapped, stuck, unable to move, and it's the feeling trapped that generates so much anger. Of course if you can feel angry you're in a better position than those that can't. It's all been sublimated and turned into something else, something so far removed from the original feeling that it's very unlikely to be recognised for what it really is without a great deal of work. Our bodies can express our anger in a variety of ways as Drs Bach and Goldberg make clear in their book *Creative Aggression*. Let me quote from a section they entitle *The Aggressive Body*:

> It is a hard clinical fact that psychosomatic syndromes do not arise when activated aggression has not been suppressed or repressed beyond a certain degree. In other words, psychosomatic diseases have repressed aggression at least as a partial cause at their root. The psychosomatic illness serves the function of warding off aggressive impulses. It arises because the person is not able to express these feelings directly... In general many psychosomatic symptoms are created when the aggressive impulse is warded off and the energy from it is being discharged into a pathway of bodily functions, rather than through open emotional responsiveness.[38]

Reconnecting with the origins of our feelings rather than meeting up with them in distorted form when they have had to find expression somatically is no easy task, not least because early emotional pathways become the template upon which we regulate our lives. However, if we wish to become more integrated and find out who we really are, then almost anything is possible. The avenues that can be the instruments for change are myriad, and may or may not involve skilled professional help, but even then only if we want to re-find our true selves and are prepared for all the inevitable upheavals that accompany profound change of this kind, challenging as it inevitably does the status quo. Anyone who has been involved in bringing about change in institutions or within themselves will know the kind of resistance I am talking about.

When a person, often quite unconsciously, has been trained by their family experience that certain emotions are dangerous, then these feelings and their expression will be taboo and forbidden. Anger is very often one of these. It holds enormous potential either to be creative or, in equal measure, to be destructive, but the latter is far more likely if the emotion has been dammed up for years, kept tied up as it were until something happens that causes it to break out. Then, like prisoners who escape, you have a riot on your hands and it feels as if all Hell has been let loose. No wonder anger gets such a bad name! Anger gone mad and out of control can, it's true, lead to murder. Equally, anger ignored and banished to the depths within us is murderous in a different way, killing off vitality and life and contributing to the sense of deadness we were thinking about earlier. The softly-spoken person whom you have to strain to hear speaking is very often deeply angry. However, harness that energy and use it constructively and it can be used to facilitate communication that really can make a difference.

Ultimately, that is what we need to achieve between the different elements within ourselves, so that new possibilities are opened up and things previously out of reach and deemed impossible now come within our grasp. Goals can be realised and the desires of our hearts can become reality rather than just the stuff of our dreams. We discover that good things can be for us and not just for others.

Anger and its expression 'or not' has so many different faces and it is these that I want us to think about as part of improving the communication within ourselves. When we can be in better communication with ourselves, we are usually in better communication with others. This is an element of what I believe it means to love ourselves as a preliminary to loving our neighbour. Unpacking that statement of Jesus has ever unfolding truths to yield. Being in better communication with ourselves is likely to mean there is a greater chance that ultimately we will experience greater contentment in living, and of course it opens the possibility for so many more choices to be available. There are less areas off-limits so to speak. A pleasant by-product of improving the relationship we have with ourselves is the transformation of loneliness into solitude, the latter being something about an enjoyment of being alone but not lonely. Henri Nouwen spoke of solitude as being 'the furnace of transformation', the place where there is space for things to happen. Creativity of any kind needs space in order to flourish and allowing the creative spirit within us to be able to work is no different.

As we increasingly attend to ourselves, we start to become more in tune with that most precious of all instruments – ourselves. An instrument that is in tune is both more enjoyable to play, as well as to be in close proximity to. I recall recently watching with awe a young girl of fifteen playing her violin for the *BBC Young Musician of the Year Competition*. She had been able to borrow a Stradivarius. To see this young girl so in tune with her instrument was profoundly moving. She touched us all by her ability to make music and not surprisingly won the competition. Interestingly, when afterwards she was interviewed prior to knowing the judges' final verdict, she remarked that for her to play such a beautiful instrument was enough, whether or not she won. This 'at home-ness' with her instrument showed in the way she played. She and her instrument moved in harmony. It was as if she and her violin engaged in a dance of making music together. Her ability to be so comfortable with her instrument added enormously to her enjoyment in playing – and ours in the listening – as well as affecting the quality of the tune that emerged. That's what I mean about being in tune with our bodies. Living and 'playing our instrument', becomes so enjoyable that winning or losing becomes irrelevant. And this ability to be in tune with the Stradivarius that is our body is a gift that is within the reach of all of us.

The complimentary healer, David Furlong picks up this theme when he speaks about the Symphony of the Self. He writes:

> If any note on the piano is sounded, the string sets up a resonating vibration that causes the corresponding octave notes also to vibrate. If you play the middle C, every other C note across all the octaves would start to sound. Indeed within musical theory and experience, playing one note causes the harmonic notes also to sound. In this sense playing a note causes energy to be transferred across all the octaves of the piano.
>
> Understanding how this process works is one of the key elements for appreciating why psychosomatic problems occur, for negative thought patterns cause corresponding imbalances at a physical level. Conversely, food, drugs and other substances introduced into the body can affect your emotions and your mind. There is a symphony playing within all parts of you at each

> moment of time. The key to life is allowing all your notes to play in tune, and what is more important, to play the music that is truly you.[39]

Discovering the uniqueness of our music is the lifelong task of us all, and the road that makes this possible is a willingness to feel what we feel rather than pretending we don't or in some other way denying our emotions. We may fool ourselves for a time, but it's a path that leads to trouble sooner or later and, more importantly, affects the quality of living open to us. It also takes a huge toll on our bodies, which bear the brunt of carrying feelings that need to be discharged through other, more appropriate channels.

So what do our bodies do when feelings that we cannot express get trapped inside us? The feelings get somatised, and the body carries the feelings. As Joyce McDougall puts it, 'When we, for any reason, fail to create some form of mental management to deal with psychic pain, psychosomatic process may take over.'[40] Our somatised feelings can come out in any number of ways. The common expressions 'a raging headache' or 'thumping head' give us useful information and suggest we might be up-tight about something. Hypertension is about high blood pressure. What, it might be wondered, is the pressure that has built up to such dangerous proportions? Or we hear of an irritable bowel, which gives away important clues as to the irritation about something which might underlie a distressing condition. What about 'explosive diarrhoea' or 'a pain in the neck', both familiar expressions that need no translation, but express so eloquently an underlying emotional trigger. I have heard it said many times that psychosomatic illness 'is all in the mind' as if it had somehow all been made up. Nothing could be further from the truth. It is very much in the body and not in the least a product of anybody's imagination. Very often the psychosomatic expression of psychic pain is intense as the feelings are getting distorted into and through the body. The pain is also very often from a time in our lives when there were no words because we had not as yet learnt to speak. Infants communicate a great deal through their bodies and rely on an adult care-giver who can make sense of their distress intuitively and take steps to alleviate it in an appropriate way.

Our minds and our bodies are very much linked and therefore

it is not surprising that feelings which for various reasons cannot find expression emotionally, often find somatic channels to express themselves through. Medication has its place, ideally alongside an exploration into the underlying emotional factors that are likely playing a part. Perhaps one could consider what this particular symptom means for this particular person at this time in their lives? What purpose does it serve and what is it in the service of? By somatising powerful and often frightening feelings, did it make them more acceptable and therefore more manageable within a particular family? These are the kind of questions we need to be asking if we want to unravel what a particular symptom might express.

The patterns for this way of relating get laid down long before any of us have rational thought and often before words are even an option, which is why it is so important to attend to thoughts and fantasies and picture images when trying to unravel and attend to somatic distress. It is a way of connecting the mind-body link. Our bodies will very often speak through colours and images and dreams. 'Dreams are intra-psychic communications that reveal in metaphorical form certain truths about the life of the dreamer, truths that can be made available to the dreamer awake.'[41] Dreams can be a real gift from our deeper selves to give us clues as to what might be going on in the deeper levels of our minds. It can also sometimes prove very enlightening to have a dialogue with the part of the body that is in pain and see what it has to say. It is also usually significant to think about when the symptom first started and what was happening for that person around that time. It all gives important clues that can help piece together the body's expression of dis-ease.

In the following chapter, as we think about the faces of anger, we will consider how some of these expressions of anger present themselves, and how our bodies very often serve as the conduit for an emotion that has high voltage energy.

## Notes

[22] 1 Corinthians 6:19

[23] Judith Hubback writing in her paper *Body Language and the Self: The search for Psychic Truth*, taken from *The Body in Analysis*, edited by Nathan Schwartz-Salant and Murray Stein, Chiron Publications, USA, 1986, p.129

[24] Brian Broom, *Somatic Illness and the Patients other Story*, Free Association Books Ltd, 1997, pp.171/172

[25] Joyce McDougall, *The Psychosoma and the Psychoanalytic Process*, from a contribution to a Symposium in Paris, 1974, p.441

[26] Joyce McDougall, *The Psychosoma and the Psychoanalytic Process*, Paris, 1974, p.458

[27] Elliott Jaques from his paper, 'Death and the Midlife Crisis', *International Journal of Psychoanalysis*, Dec 10, 1990, p.508

[28] Mathew, Sheila and Dennis Linn, *Healing Religious Addiction*, Darton, Longman and Todd, 1995, p.11

[29] Luke 6:41

[30] David Furlong, *The Healer Within: How to Awaken and Develop your Healing Potential*, Piatkus, London, 1995, 1998, 1999(twice), p.81

[31] Luke 8:46

[32] Joyce McDougall, *The Psychosoma and the Psychoanalytic Process*, from a contribution to a Symposium in Paris, 1974, p.445

[33] Martin Smith, *The World is Very Near You*, Darton, Longman and Todd, 1989, p.97

[34] Margaret Magdalen CSMV, *The Hidden Face of Jesus*, Darton, Longman and Todd, London, 1994, p.193

[35] M Scott Peck, *The Road Less Travelled*, Hutchinson and Co., 1983, p.158, Arrow Books, 1990

[36] Freud, 'The Unconscious', 1915 b, in Vol. 14 of *The Complete Works of Sigmund Freud*, Hogarth Press, London, 1963, p.194

[37] Neville Symington, *The Making of a Psychotherapist*, Karnac Books Ltd, 1996, p.16

[38] Dr George R Bach and Dr Herb Goldberg, *Creative Aggression – The Art of Assertive Living*, Coventure, London, 1974, p.232

[39] David Furlong, *The Healer Within*, Piatkus Publishers Ltd, 1995, pp.23/24

[40] Joyce McDougall, *The Psychosoma and the Psychoanalytic Process*, Paris, 1974, p.439

[41] Margaret Arden, *Midwifery of the Soul*, from her paper *Dreamwork beyond Psychoanalysis*, Free Association Books Ltd, 1998, p.93

## Faces of Anger

Anger is like a multi-faceted jewel, revealing different aspects of itself according to how you see it, and from which direction the light shines. I want in this chapter for us to think about some of the many faces of anger, as part of enlarging our understanding of it. However, it is important that we first establish that anger is a natural response to needs not being met, with all the attendant hurt that such a situation arouses – particularly if these things happened at a time in our lives when we were dependant upon our primary care-givers to provide these things for us. All feelings are valid. The only point where right or wrong comes into it is in what we do with our feelings. Some responses are more helpful than others, and in this chapter the focus will tend to be on less helpful expressions of anger, whilst the next chapter focuses more on creative ways of using anger.

What immediately comes to mind is the disguised face of anger, which necessarily underlies all the other manifestations of anger, the aim of which is to disguise it from ourselves. If we can tell ourselves it isn't anger, or locate it in something or someone else, then inevitably it distances us from that feeling, and for a while, we feel more comfortable. In one form or another this enables us to hide an emotion that for a variety of reasons is felt to be too frightening to tolerate consciously. Anger and its derivatives can be felt to be so frightening that the feeling has to be warded off, either by repressing it at source, which the unconscious part of our mind does for us so that we don't even have to think about it, or suppressing it with a more conscious mechanism. We manage to pretend it's not there by hiding it. However, other forces within us sometimes let the cat out of the bag as the following example from Scott Peck's work as a psychiatrist and psychotherapist illustrates.

> A meticulous woman, totally unable to acknowledge in herself

the emotion of anger and therefore unable to express anger openly, began a pattern of arriving a few minutes late for her therapy sessions. I suggested to her that this was because she was feeling some resentment toward me or toward therapy or both. She firmly denied this was a possibility, explaining that her lateness was purely a matter of this or that accidental force in life and proclaiming her wholehearted appreciation of me and motivation for our work together. On the evening following this session she paid her monthly bills, including my own. Her cheque to me arrived unsigned. At her next session I informed her of this, suggesting again that she had not paid me properly because she was angry. She said, 'But that's ridiculous! I have never in my life not signed a cheque. You know how meticulous I am in these matters. It is impossible that I did not sign your cheque.' I showed her the unsigned cheque. Although she had always been extremely controlled in our sessions, she now suddenly broke into sobs. 'What is happening to me?' she wailed. 'I'm falling apart. It's like I'm two people.' In her agony, and with my acknowledgement that she was indeed like a house divided against itself, she began for the first time to accept the possibility that at least a part of her might harbor the feeling of anger.[42]

It makes a lot of sense that if we are unable to tolerate a particular emotion, it will find other ways to come out. Projection is one such mechanism, safely distancing us from the emotion that we find so difficult to assimilate. Our anger gets projected into something or someone else, generally someone whose early experience has unconsciously trained them to carry anger for the family and who are therefore equipped for this role. So for example, you have an exemplary family with morally upright parents who are recognised as absolute pillars of society, esteemed by everyone, but one of their children behaves entirely out of character with the family ethos. Aggressive, unruly, either constantly in trouble with society or compliantly fitting in outwardly but paying a heavy price inwardly. The cost will not infrequently manifest itself in illness as the only acceptable way the family difficulty can find expression. By this time the feeling may well have been sublimated into something else altogether. Whichever, it is the same mechanism that is operating. Anger is felt to be too difficult an emotion to handle and has to be 'got rid of by any means possible. People are not the only recipients of anger. Very often it gets displaced onto animals or objects in the environment. Kicking the door or the metaphorical cat will be familiar concepts.

In families where it is felt to be too frightening for angry feelings to be comfortably accepted and managed, something has to be done to remove it from conscious awareness. This might be by unconsciously putting it into one of their children, for example, where it is at a sufficiently safe distance from them as to no longer be a part of them, but out there belonging to someone else. In this case, the unfortunate child who may well be criticised for sulking, being rude, unco-operative, or any of the other ways that any of us find when struggling with an emotion that we feel unable to externalise in any other way. Or it all gets taken out on oneself in self-destructive behaviours designed at obtaining relief. If it is really taboo within a particular family, the child can't even have the relief of being naughty and acting it out in that way, and so tries ever harder to be the exemplary child, swallowing all the corporate family anger as well as their own, until it finds some other way out that is more acceptable to all concerned, such as illness. After all, if the child is by now displaying signs of illness, he or she can be taken to the doctor, which quite apart from anything else now means that their problem has become someone else's, and what's more, it's no longer within the family but posed as a problem for the doctor, the hospital, them out there to solve. The doctor and group analyst Robin Skynner, in a collection of papers about individual, group and family therapy, has this to say in relation to this matter:

> I have been impressed with the constant finding that disturbed marriages are haunted by disturbing internalised parental figures, and that many less viable marriages – perhaps those most likely to break up – have occurred in an attempt to render more manageable hateful parental introjects which show similar features in both partners, and which each partner previously found even more difficult to cope with on his own. Sometimes, each partner will keep his or her own ghostly persecutor safely contained in the spouse, with inevitable mutual rejection and attack, as well as equally inevitable inability to separate. Other

couples form a tight alliance in order to keep the dreaded shared internal figure projected into a scapegoated child, or outside the family altogether into a generally persecuting world.[43]

In the current political climate as manifested on the world scene, that last phrase has a disturbing familiarity about it. As a tactic for evasion it is effective in the short term, but is in all other respects disastrous. The child (or community) is overloaded with an emotion that is considered to be very bad, with no appropriate way of expressing and discharging it. A possible scenario is that the angry feelings get acted out in violent behaviours. To return to the family scene that Skynner was mentioning, where angry feelings from the adults are displaced into a child, the parents are at the very least, depleted of a rich source of energy and relational communication, not to mention the effect such unconscious manipulation might have on the family dynamics in general. Imagine the impact for a child to feel it has so much of something that its family feel is bad? So bad that it must never be spoken about or shared. Inevitably the child absorbs a sense that he or she must be bad, and there the seeds are lain for a poor self-image and low self-esteem. The repercussions of which may well dog them for the rest of their lives to a greater or lesser degree, depending on whether they discover a capacity to modify it or not. Skynner talks about feelings being projected into a scapegoated child, which is a theme Scott Peck elaborates on in some depth in his book *People of the Lie*. He writes,

> A predominant characteristic of the behaviour of those I call evil, is scapegoating. Scapegoating works through the mechanism of projection. Since they must deny their own badness, they perceive others as bad. They project their own evil onto the world. Evil then is most often committed in order to scapegoat, and the people I label as evil are chronic scapegoaters. The evil attack others instead of facing their own failures.
>
> The words 'image', 'appearance', 'outwardly' are crucial to understanding the morality of the evil. While they seem to lack any motivation to be good, they intensely desire to appear good. Their goodness is all on a level of pretence. It is in effect a lie.
>
> The lie is designed not so much to deceive others, as to deceive themselves. They cannot or will not tolerate the pain of

> self-reproach. The decorum with which they lead their lives is maintained as a mirror in which they can see themselves reflected righteously. They feel themselves to be perfect.
>
> The lie can be perceived before the misdeed it is designed to hide – the cover up before the fact. We see the smile that hides the hatred, the smooth oily manner that masks the fury, the velvet glove that covers the fist.[44]

Scott Peck leaves us in no doubt how strongly he feels about people who use the mechanism of projection, and whilst I agree with him that to attribute feelings that belong to ourselves onto others is a form of evil, particularly when that person may well be a vulnerable person such as a child, we also need to recognise that this capacity for evil lies within all of us, and developed in the first place because anger in the original family setting was taboo. What do any of us do when one road is blocked? We find another way, which projection provides. Anyone in a position of leadership, and therefore authority, can very easily become the focus for projections. Sandler comments on this: 'Clearly politicians frequently serve as the target for the projection of a variety of wishes and affects which the projector cannot directly express or even consciously tolerate within himself.'[45]

When we have to see ourselves as above reproach and cannot tolerate being seen to have made a mistake or got it wrong, then we are vulnerable to projecting our shadow side onto others. The reason of course is that to do so involves experiencing the feelings, rather than distancing oneself from them and locating them instead in someone else who is then both left with the problem and becomes seen as the problem. Maybe we need to remember that it is our shadow that gives us such depth and character, and that to project those aspects of ourselves into someone else, albeit unconsciously, is to deprive ourselves of such a rich source of emotional currency.

The family is the first group that any of us experience, and those early dynamics have a tendency to keep recurring in any group setting, whatever the particular context. The psychiatrist and psychotherapist Thomas H Ogden has written a fascinating book about these projective processes. I quote from his discoveries about group interaction on an in-patient ward to illustrate the concepts we have been thinking about.

> It has become a cliché to say that a given member of a group may voice or enact the feelings of the entire group without being aware that he is doing so. But what is meant by that? How has the given group member ceased to speak or behave as an individual and instead come to function as the vehicle for the expression of collective feelings? I feel that when people talk in these terms they are talking about projective identification in a group setting. For a great many reasons, usually having to do with the individual dynamics of the group members involved, a given set of feelings arising in a group setting is felt to be unacceptable and intolerable, and there is the wish on the part of many or all of the members of the group to get rid of these feelings. The group then polarises into two partially separate psychological functions, with one part of the group functioning as the projector, and the other part of the group, often a single person, functioning as the recipient. The projectors feel a bond with each other, since they all unconsciously imagine that they have rid themselves of an unwanted, unacceptable aspect of themselves. There is often a sense of virtuousness among those serving as projectors. In contrast the recipient is viewed – and unconsciously experiences himself – as a container of the expelled, unacceptable feelings and attributes with which the group is collectively preoccupied. Pressure is exerted on the recipient to behave and experience himself only in a manner that is congruent with the shared projective fantasy.[46]

It is not difficult to see that dumping one's emotional rubbish into someone else may for the time being make us feel better, because we have got rid of something we don't want. We feel relieved. However, it is also not difficult to see the effect of this indiscriminate dumping on the unfortunate recipient, who gets increasingly bad tempered or sick until their snapping point is reached. The emotional bucket has reached the limits of its capacity to contain any more and breakdown of some kind ensues.

The tragedy about this kind of scenario is that emotional patterns have been laid down in the formative years of our lives and set the scene for the kind of interactions we habitually tend to recreate in adult life. This occurs very often in the way that we are all powerfully influenced at an unconscious level, as to who we choose as friends or life partner, the scene is set for us to recreate our early life training in adult relationships. The reason for this is that within all of us is a healing potential that wants to recreate in order to resolve. Seen from this perspective, current dilemmas and conflicts can take on a more creative possibility. For example, the person who has been exposed to this kind of psychological transaction early on, is very vulnerable to being used by others. They may end up choosing a partner who needs someone to carry their anger for them, or someone who will habitually do all the work clearing up after them. Whenever I see household rubbish dumped in lay-bys or at the edge of waste ground, I am reminded of this kind of emotional dumping.

People vulnerable to being unconsciously used in this way will do anything for anyone, generally taking on the tasks no-one else wants to do and thereby earning a few crumbs of approval from important others in their community. It is a familiar place for them emotionally. They are unable to say no and so tend to get all sorts dumped on them. They like to please and nothing is too much trouble, or so it seems. However, after a time, which may extend into many years, they may tire of being a dogsbody or feeling like a doormat for all and sundry to wipe their metaphorical feet on. They may start to have feelings of wishing they could have a less demanding and exhausting kind of life, because all this feeling not unlike a slave is very tiring. Exhausting, in a word, and not much fun either. They may well feel very resentful about such a situation, and probably envious of those who don't seem to have to take on the world in quite such a demanding way. It is unlikely any of this can be voiced for fear of reprisals and the feared loss of the approval they crave. It takes more than a few weeks or months of skilled professional therapeutic help to repair this kind of damage, as part of changing well-established patterns of relating, the roots of which go back into earliest experiences.

Not infrequently it can reach back over several generations, getting more and more reinforced with every successive generation, until something happens in the life of the last member in the family chain who, for whatever reason, cannot any longer contain so much unexpressed emotion and breaks down under the strain. The metaphorical dam holding all this dammed-up emotion bursts under the pressure, causing untold damage both to the dam and to the surrounding environment, which will inevitably be caught up in the flood that ensues. As any water authority will tell you, when the pressure is rising within the dam it is prudent to release it safely by opening the sluice gates in a controlled and monitored way. The templates for living, which we all inherit, can be reset more appropriately as we consciously re-examine our ways of being in the world and make important decisions as to whether or not they are still serving us helpfully.

Managing our emotions to get the most out of life is what this is all about so that we feel more in control of them, rather than the other way around – which is what happens in the negative group projective processes that we were thinking about earlier. In a very real sense our feelings are the tools we have been given for living, and they are all there inside for our benefit. They provide us with useful information about the situations we find ourselves in, what we like and dislike, what we want and don't want, what we love and want more of, our needs and hungers. The latter are sometimes referred to in some circles in such a way as to imply that to have needs is a crime. Having needs is part of being human, and as we all share the experience of having been born as helpless, dependant infants, we all have needs, even if some people in later life defend themselves vigorously against being dependant upon anyone ever again, because at some earlier stage they have been so let down and so hurt. It is true we cannot always have everything we want when we want it, but if our disappointment about that can be acknowledged and legitimate needs met consistently, confidence grows that they will continue to be met, ultimately by ourselves for ourselves. The child, and the child part of all of us, is more able to relax in the security of that situation, and can get on with living and growing, playing and generally enjoying life. This is unlike the experience of early deprivation, where the whole focus of life becomes a preoccupation with survival and trying to meet needs from within oneself, which as children we are not psychologically equipped to manage. As adults the hungry parts of ourselves need to know we will not be ignored, but attended to lovingly and consistently on a regular basis. And predominantly that caring attitude needs to be what each of us develops towards the vulnerable parts of ourselves.

We may recall experiences of being with certain individuals who are emotionally very hungry but unable to nurture themselves, with the result that they have a tendency to latch on to others emotionally, rather as parasites do to their host. After any length of time in their presence one can become aware of feeling increasingly drained and depleted, suggesting that a kind of emotional exchange has gone on. The giveaway is that after a time, one begins to feel enervated, while they seem to become increasingly energised and full of life. Feeling that someone has robbed us of our vitality is bound to generate angry feelings. Not for nothing we might catch ourselves after such an experience using the colloquial phrase 'so-and-so has sucked me dry.' The body, as we were reflecting on earlier, has very descriptive ways of telling us exactly what has been going on. Creeping Ivy knows which trees are worthy of latching on to in order to feed off the trees' sap. A similar situation can arise where a person feels so empty that they unconsciously latch on to those who they see as having vitality and resilience and plenty of life about them, and take it from them. In the same way that ivy knows which tree will be a worthy host, so in the signals we are all communicating all the time we may, without having realised it, have conveyed a receptiveness to serving as the host for others to feed off. It has to be acknowledged that this is never a one-way process. At some level, if we find ourselves in such a situation, we have contributed to it. Maybe it makes us feel good to help someone, maybe we like the affirmation, feeling wanted. It vicariously meets a need in us, because of course while it is allowed and possibly even encouraged, there is a huge pay-off from the other, in terms of friendship, gratitude, appreciation, approval, affirmation – probably all the things that have been in short supply earlier in the formative years of our lives. It is not difficult to see how vulnerable to such a dynamic we are, if unmet needs are powerfully propelling us in this direction.

I recall walking along a river bank on one occasion in Devon and seeing several trees that had been taken over by ivy to such an extent that they were leaning heavily under the pressure. Unable to remain standing, some had fallen to the point where they were very obviously dying. It was a shocking example of what can happen when ivy is left to take over a tree, and its obvious parallel in our own lives when we allow others to feed off us indiscriminately, or what we could inadvertently cause to someone else as a consequence of not attending to ourselves. The person concerned may be unaware of what they are doing and the effect they might be having on us, but once we have become aware of what is going on it is our responsibility to protect ourselves. This will involve looking at our part in the dynamic between us, it may be by setting limits on how much time we spend with them, by communicating in various ways that we are not open to being used in this way or, in some situations, it may be that certain relationships are not healthy for us to continue with.

Other examples of anger being distanced from its original feeling include someone saying they have had a flare up of their irritable bowel syndrome, or they have had an asthmatic attack, or they'll find relief in self-harming behaviour and cut themselves, or more commonly describe themselves as having a raging headache. It will be seen how the body does in fact describe very clearly to us what is going on, once we have the ears to hear it. The body feels it for us and expresses it somatically. Our minds are very much part of our bodies and therefore it is entirely natural that what can't find expression in one realm, will find an outlet in the other. As Neville Symington puts it, 'a psychological stoppage usually manifests itself in the somatic sphere.'[47]

Envy is a particular face of anger that isn't always recognised as even being associated with anger. Classified in some circles as one of the seven deadly sins, it is hastily banished. It is very closely allied with anger – inevitably, as envy is about lack and wanting what someone else has got but feeling there is no possibility of ever having the good thing for oneself. Such a situation is guaranteed to generate angry feelings, however much they may be denied. It also sets up the kind of situations we have been thinking about. After all, if someone else has something that you would love but feel is denied to you, then the good thing gets taken covertly and without permission. People steal when they haven't the resources for what they want, and feel there could never be any possibility of discovering such resources, especially from within themselves. The motive may change, in that for some, stealing is about revenge, a sort of 'if I can't have it then you can't either,' but at bottom it's about wanting something and feeling that it is completely out of reach. Whole new vistas open up when we begin to see that good and desired things can be for us, as well as others.

The word envy is derived from the Latin word *Invedere*, meaning to look into. Where envy is around there is a great preoccupation with what others have, and what others think. Comparisons are constantly and unhelpfully being made, and one senses the competing and rivalry which have all the hallmarks of envy. Envy gets its bad reputation because of the destructiveness associated with it, but envy can also be a springboard to growth if we can emulate and work towards having the desired attribute. Imagine how different it could feel to realise at a deeply emotional level, rather than just intellectually, that you can have good things and so can I. In other words one doesn't have to be at the expense of the other. We would all probably ascribe to this apparently simple statement at an intellectual level, but earlier parts of ourselves sometimes need a lot of help in making that connection and working it through sufficiently so that it becomes a part of our thinking and way of being in the world. That kind of thinking opens up a whole new world of possibilities – but not before a great deal of rethinking has happened to allow for such a changed perspective.

Envious feelings emanate from our earliest feelings of lack, at a stage in our lives when we were helpless and dependant on others to provide for us. This is partly why the emotion generates such strong feelings, because for that early part of us there was no possibility of feeling we could get what we needed and wanted. How different then when as adults we have the ability to meet our own needs and can move from a position of helplessness to one of autonomy. The desired thing is no longer felt to be unobtainable, but within reach for us to work towards.

Where envy is influencing how we relate, there is huge guilt about having nice things for oneself and a pressure from within to justify any aberration from living frugally. It is not difficult to see how this perpetuates the very emptiness that lies at the heart of the problem, and sets up situations where good things can only be sneaked or stolen in some way, or gained vicariously through others, posing as a very counterfeit kind of goodness. That kind of goodness, which is all about feeding oneself, is especially repellent. I recall several years ago, whilst working within a pastoral setting in a church community, having invitations to coffee. On the face of it these seemed generous gestures but somehow I found myself feeling increasingly irritated by them. Only when I wondered why such apparent kindness was irritating me so much did I realise that these invitations were not about a mutual enjoyment of one another's company, but to facilitate an opportunity for them to have my undivided attention for an hour in order to offload their problems, whilst hiding behind the guise of being friendly. If they could have been honest and said, 'I'm worried about… Could we find a time to meet and talk about it?', I would have felt very differently. Instead I felt manipulated, used and irritated, until I was able to process my anger sufficiently to discover what was going on and use the insights gained from within myself to deal with the situation differently.

Where envy is operating unhelpfully by keeping us depleted and empty, it sets up situations within ourselves whereby we find it difficult to allow ourselves to have anything good, what the psychoanalyst Barry Proner refers to as 'envy of the self'. It is a difficult concept to grasp, but essentially is about an attacking part of our mental apparatus that attempts to keep the healthier parts of ourselves from having anything good, so maintaining the inner emptiness and deprivation and therefore keeping things the same, which threatens no-one and is 'safe'. So for example, we attribute all our good qualities as belonging to others and have difficulty owning them as our own, fearing that we are being big headed or arrogant.

It can be seen that one of the functions of this way of being is an attempt to protect the good thing from envious attack, because at some level there is the unconscious realisation that having good things and good experiences provokes this internal attack and spoils it. So if we unconsciously decide to locate our strengths in others, it protects us from the feared envy, but of course it also depletes us of a very essential part of ourselves. Can we not recall from the wellsprings of our own experience occasions when having acquired something particularly nice, we suffered guilty feelings of a particularly pernicious kind? Does this not lie behind a curious mechanism whereby we buy something new and then end up taking it back to the shop? Compliments cannot be enjoyed and used to feed us from within, but get rubbished or in some way watered down; 'he didn't really mean it' or 'I wonder what she wants', rather than being able to enjoy the good experience and allowing it to nourish us from inside. Another common way that the good thing is diminished is when someone speaks affirmingly of something we have achieved, and we remark, 'it's nothing.' A classic example of the way it is so often we ourselves who contribute to our own suffering. The good thing gets made null and void and turned into nothing. It can be seen how this fuels our emptiness and sets us up to unconsciously attract the negative from others, because as part of not feeling we are entitled to good things, our life set has primed us to believe good things are only for others, whether material, emotional or spiritual. We erroneously believe at some much deeper level within us that we are destined to contain the bad, not just our own but everyone else's too. Others pick up these unconscious signals, which ensures we remain depleted of good things by siphoning off our good qualities and exchanging them with their negative aspects for us to look after.

Maggie Scarf, in her excellent book *Intimate Partners*, talks about the mechanism of projection between couples and has this to say:

> What must be held firmly in mind – for it is of vital significance – is that when partners collude to re-create charged aspects of the past, it is never a one-way process; it is not in other words something that one member of the couple does to the other. On the contrary, two motivated players must be involved; otherwise the collusive game will never get going.[48]

So what might it mean to feel that there is an alternative to having perpetually to feel depleted and empty? What immediately comes to mind is that one no longer has to fill up the emptiness inside with the negative. We can begin to feed ourselves emotionally and retain the good things, rather than metaphorically spitting them out, as for example when we negate compliments. I have noticed a spiritualised version of this when in response to any significant achievement, the satisfaction and pleasure is attributed to God as if He might in some way be threatened and not approve of one's abilities and aptitudes. I have done so myself and came to see that this was much more about deflecting the feared envy from others about my achievement. We need to wonder where such conditioned thinking comes from, and was God being cast in a particular role that perhaps had much more to do with significant figures in our formative years than with God?

I had someone to visit recently who was admiring the daffodils in my kitchen, and commented that she never felt able to buy flowers for herself, and always felt she had to wait in the hope that someone would buy some for her. I encouraged her to feel she could have, and deserved to have, good things for herself and that maybe buying some flowers for herself would be a good start. She liked the idea so I hope she allowed the thought to develop sufficiently to bring about what she wanted. A simple shift in thinking that could have far-reaching implications both for her and those around her, who at some level pick up the feeling that something is expected of them when they visit and after a time come to resent it. Seemingly insignificant conversations can sometimes take us by surprise in the impact they have. Oak trees grow from acorns that fall on receptive soil.

This business of retaining good things has all sorts of repercussions. Compliments can be received and not just tolerated but enjoyed, rather than immediately spat out, admiring looks can be a source of pleasure rather than experienced as 'someone looking at me critically', new clothes can be chosen and worn with joy rather than immediately spoilt and sabotaged with guilt and endless justification about having been acquired in the sales, the charity shop or as a gift. Second-hand clothes no longer have to dominate the wardrobe – not that there is anything wrong with this form of re-cycling. It is much more about understanding the meaning behind what we do and what it is in the service of. Maybe there is the feeling one can only justify having something for oneself if it is second-hand. And for someone who feels uncomfortable about having new things, the charity shop can justify the longing for something new, especially as the money is going to a good cause. This is doubly valuable if we feel we don't deserve new things for ourselves. The work of Creation and the world of nature frequently reminds me of the lavish generosity of God, who was Himself able to say after each day's created work 'and it was very good.'[49] It feels not insignificant that the Bible starts with an account of God's capacity for enjoyment and pleasure in His creativity. Envy destroys joy and enjoyment of all good things, breaking up the good experience until it is suitably mashed up and unrecognisable for what it had been. The compliment that started off as something so pure and beautiful, gets reduced to 'she didn't really mean it.'

This mechanism can be seen operating in the area of holidays too. 'Far too decadent to allow oneself such luxuries as a week or two off!' says envy. When we are in the grip of envy, anything as potentially lovely as a good holiday becomes a target for the feared internal reprisals. If it can be linked in some way for the benefit of others it eases that critical voice from within that immediately threatens to spoil the thought of a holiday by whispering 'how selfish' or 'what will so and so think?', or even worse 'what will happen to so and so', which inevitably adds guilt into the thought processes. Not difficult to understand why any of us might dissipate these inner attacks by getting involved in facilitating holidays for others, as that then justifies it for us. The tyrant within us can be appeased with the thought that such benevolence is for others not for us. We may fall prey to blaming insufficient finance as a reason why we cannot indulge in nice holidays, which of course is trying to justify primarily to ourselves, and ease our own disappointment and envy of others who can. I still recall the hoops I had to pass through to have our first proper holiday. But then, as we were seeing earlier, having a holiday is something that can be seen by others and therefore commented upon, whereas spending money on acquiring equipment of one sort or another at home is rather more private and unseen. As we all know, holidays do not have to be exorbitant, which such all-or-nothing thinking turns it into, thus justifying why such an indulgence can't be afforded. It is often much more about not feeling able to allow ourselves time out, time to relax, time just to 'be', rather than the constant pressure from within ourselves to continuously and compulsively be busy, along with the punishing guilt that gives any of us a hard time if we let up even for a moment. It can be a very important and significant development when we see what we have been doing to ourselves and recognise the power of these dynamics to hold us back from enjoying life.

Facilitating a holiday for others or signing up as a helper on holidays for the disadvantaged can be the only way some people struggling with this internal conflict can justify, primarily to themselves, their wish to have a break. Facilitating good things for others are all worthy things, I hasten to add, but what I am hoping to highlight is our motive in doing what we do, so that we don't kid ourselves, and more importantly the people who we are involving ourselves with. Few things are more irksome than feeling someone is doing us good when primarily it is for their benefit. Of course, in any helping capacity, we are inevitably doing ourselves good, but as I mentioned earlier, it has a different quality about it when we can acknowledge that the currency is very much two-way. Others cannot allow themselves the holiday unless they take someone who needs looking after and who may well drain them in the process, about which they may feel resentful at some level, but feel at a loss as to how they can overcome the inner blocks to allowing themselves what they may desperately want and need, but cannot as yet feel able to have. It is not difficult to see why any of us might be envious of those that can, if this particular conflict is still causing us a destructive amount of stress. In this way the potential value and enjoyment of any holiday gets sabotaged. It is felt unconsciously that there is a price to pay for wanting something for ourselves – and then unwittingly it is we who exact the price upon ourselves. Another example of how we contribute to our own suffering.

When this face of anger is operating, there is always a price to be paid. Good things cannot be enjoyed and end up being sabotaged and spoilt. Envy is one of the most terrible and deadly faces of anger because of its capacity to spoil. This can even operate at such a basic level as food, where nice meals can only be justified if visitors are present. In other words, the effort and the expense is for others (of course) and not ourselves – though let us not deceive ourselves. In these circumstances we enjoy the meal vicariously because it is safe. I can still recall the ambivalence I felt about having a nice meal and not a visitor in sight! Let it also be acknowledged that achieving a significant change of attitude once does not overnight change the habits of a lifetime – but it's a very important first step, demonstrating that change is possible, and giving the kind of encouragement necessary to allow further changes to happen as part of establishing new ways of thinking and being.

In time we can be helped to realise that good things are permitted and are to be encouraged for the sheer enjoyment of the experience. Our having something doesn't have to be at the cost of others going without, or that we have set ourselves up to be attacked in some way. It can be very salutary when we realise that the reprisals and fears of attack is what primarily goes on in our own thinking. Envy resides in all of us, however much we may try to deny its existence in ourselves. The creative side of envy is that it can be a springboard to attaining the desired thing for oneself, but for that to happen our envy needs to have become something we can be aware of consciously. It is when it is affecting us unconsciously that it can be so destructive as this excerpt from Neville Symington makes clear:

> If I say to a friend: 'I do envy you, your ability to learn languages so easily,' then here is something conscious and manageable which can even be a spur to me to emulate him. However, if I say bitterly of this same friend something like: 'John only pretends he can speak many languages,' then I am expressing unconscious envy.
>
> I went to a conference, one where someone gave a very good paper on a therapeutic subject from a cross-cultural angle. An excellent paper, it was derived from the lecturer's own experience of working within a particular working class culture; I had never heard a better paper on the subject. As I came out of the lecture hall I found myself brushing shoulders with someone who fancied himself in the same field as the lecturer. 'Excellent paper, wasn't it?' I said to him, and my interlocutor replied with barely concealed contempt: 'I suppose he had read a lot.' I am sure that the lecturer had indeed read quite widely, but the source of the

paper was in his own experience, daring and creativity. It was this that my acquaintance could not bear.[50]

However, for the destructively envious person, such a shift in thinking hasn't yet happened because they have not felt able to own this aspect of themselves. So rather than feeling they could work towards the desired thing or their own version of what they want, they feel impotent and angry. It is just such anger that lies behind the envious attacks that can be felt to be so deadly poisonous. The biting remarks about another's good fortune, the cutting comment that crushes another's enjoyment of what they have achieved, spoiling it for them and at some level easing very slightly the perpetrator's envy. It's an example of the comment I made earlier whereby the thinking is 'if I can't have it I shall make sure you can't either'. And of course, as I referred to earlier, envious attacks are not just limited to their external manifestation. They happen within us. You may be quite sure that where the envious face of anger is operating, there is an equal or greater degree of envy directed internally against oneself.

How can this be, you may well be wondering? We have been speaking about the difficulty in feeling that one is allowed and entitled to have good things. That such things are not only allowed for others. The mechanism that feeds that kind of thinking and keeps it going is when a part of our psychic apparatus acts as a kind of saboteur to the rest of us, and dangles as it were the Sword of Damocles over the healthier parts of ourselves, its function being to ensure the status quo is preserved and not challenged in any way. It is this envious attacking part of ourselves that prevents the enjoyment of anything good, either prior to the anticipated good experience by filling our mind with thoughts of 'it wouldn't be right', or that such an indulgence would be selfish, or it manifests itself retrospectively in reprisals if we have managed to overcome the negative whisperings from within. For example, the compulsive habit of taking new clothes back to the shop. The reprisals take the form of crippling guilt, or that you must work harder and have been lazy, or if you have had one drink you mustn't have two – that would be deemed greedy by this part of the personality, whose sole function is to spoil and negate the good experience. And of course when this is operating it inevitably keeps the person envious of others. Not least envious of their ability to be able to enjoy life so much.

Hence, in those moments when we cannot allow ourselves to relax, we might resent those that can, coming out with martyrish comments as we busy around with whatever we feel has to be done, like 'it's all right for some'. If we cannot allow ourselves holidays there can be resentment of those who do. Or if, from internal pressures, we feel compelled to be busy and take on more and more, we resent those that don't struggle with that particular dynamic. Which takes us into the whole business of comparing and competing, which never does anyone any good, least of all ourselves.

We need to remind ourselves at such times of our common humanity, and the ebb and flow of feelings that is part of being human. In general these skills haven't been unfairly dished out, but learnt through much time and effort arising out of a profound dissatisfaction with life. This is what provides the impetus for change along with the belief that somewhere out there, there must be more to life. There is – and those willing to search will find. Curiosity can expand our horizons in untold ways as Moses long ago discovered when his curiosity led him to investigate the phenomenon of the burning bush. Ultimately it was to lead him to the Promised Land, a land we are told that symbolically flowed with milk and honey. What a wonderful picture of lavish provision! Nourishment, sweetness – elements that energise and add enjoyment to the quality of life. The good things and good experiences were there to be enjoyed again and again, with enough for all. This land symbolically resides within all of us in terms of our capacity for enjoyment, and awaits to be endlessly discovered.

That is the inheritance of us all, not just a privileged few. But we may be required to enter into a long and arduous wilderness journey in order to get there, and discover for ourselves that the wilderness in whatever form it takes, is the harbinger of life, the place of discovery, the experience of enabling that ultimately leads us to discover our own Promised Land. Those riches that are within all of us if we will take the time to look inside. The merchant man of the gospel parable had done a great deal of trading in lesser pearls in order to know when he found the real thing, the pearl of great price. And having found what he had been searching for, he was prepared to make the necessary sacrifices in order to have it for himself. We are told he was prepared to relinquish the lesser pearls in order to afford what he really wanted. That choice remains the same for us all, but in order for that to happen we have to know what we want and go for it. 'Ask,' said Jesus, 'and you will receive, seek and you will find'.[51]

In our own search for the things that truly satisfy, we will also need to relinquish those things that are unhelpful, that hold us back from becoming and being the people we are destined to be. An important element of that is the development of a searing honesty that enables us to admit to ourselves what we really feel, what we really like or dislike, as it is our feelings that serve as the beacon to guide us. Jesus, in another of his profound sayings that cut to the heart of the matter, once said, 'The Kingdom of Heaven is within you',[52] a fact that very often seems to get overlooked, as people feverishly expend untold amounts of energy trying to prepare themselves for the heaven that is associated with life after death, and in the process sometimes miss out on the joys of life before death, of what it means to discover the Kingdom of Heaven within ourselves.

Christian Aid came out with a very good advert displayed on billboards around the country and in their literature, which said 'We believe in life before death'. This is a discovery which, I hasten to add, is not a once-and-for-all discovery, but something ongoing, which unfolds as we become ready to receive the treasures within ourselves and value them. Nor is this quest to find life without its own demands, as Jesus acknowledged in the succinct way He had. 'The gate to life is narrow and the way that leads to it is hard, and there are few people who find it.'[53] An interesting observation about human nature is that most of us have a tendency to want the easy way, the wide path, so to speak, whereby we can follow the crowd. The path to life is hard because personal change is so demanding and challenging, but also very rewarding. The reward is increasingly finding life and consequently coming to life. Those words of Jesus also very much convey to me a sense of needing to discover it for ourselves rather than having it handed to us on a plate. We have to make it our own, and that only happens as we walk the road that takes us where we need to go.

Make no mistake, discovering our treasure carries with it a responsibility. Jesus had a great deal to say about people who bury their talents for fear of what might happen if they were seen and used. The envy of which we have been speaking in its more devious aspects of holding us back from becoming our true selves, has to be attended to over a long enough period of time to enable sufficient inner growth to occur, so that we are able to discover and make use of the storehouse within. It is also true that unless we are ready and able to value a particular gift we are unlikely to discover it. The somewhat startling comment of Jesus not to throw your pearls before swine who will just trample them underfoot applies not just to 'them out there' who may not value what we have to offer, but also applies very much to ourselves in terms of the value we place and demonstrate on the particular treasures and 'pearls' that we have discovered from the storehouse of treasure within ourselves. The Kingdom of Heaven is indeed within us, and how good it can feel to access this incredible resource, which, because it is inside us, is in a place where 'moth and rust cannot destroy and robbers cannot break in and steal'.[54] Sadly, part of the destructiveness of envy is its ability to corrupt and spoil and steal what is our inheritance to have and to hold and to enjoy. The seeds of it are there in all of us, and if we are to become who we have it in us to be, we need to attend to this emotion whose roots lie in our response to insufficiencies from our earliest days. Otherwise, the destructive elements within us can keep us in an endless cycle of emptiness and deprivation, and an equally endless cycle of rage about the unfairness of life. A rage that sets others up as having everything, the inference being that we have nothing. This is not true but an expression of what, for that moment in time, feels true and it feels as if there can be no hope of anything changing for the better.

What happens to all this rage that cannot find creative expression to bring about change? It can contribute significantly to depression. This is a topic about which much has been written elsewhere, but for our purposes I want to think about it briefly as another face of anger, that probably to some degree touches us all from time to time, and like a face, has many different expressions. Winston Churchill used to describe his as 'the black dog'; others refer to it as a black cloud that hangs over them in an oppressive and menacing way, and others cannot find the words to describe the terrible sensations that envelop them. We will all have our own experience of it, either fleeting or more prolonged, and our own language to help define what it means for us. A common thread in its manifestation is its capacity to depress us, i.e. to keep us down, making the effort of living feel too much. Its effects can reach into every aspect of our lives, dulling our senses, removing appetites, waking us from sleep, etc. Whatever else its meaning might be, it is literally a wake-up call from within ourselves, to make us take note that all is not well. The soul is troubled and needs to be heard and attended to. Part of that process may well be medication, but it is essential that we also understand what the depression is trying to communicate to us. It is a clarion call for us to listen, and primarily to ourselves, to whatever unease is reaching intolerable proportions within us.

It feels important at this point that we also acknowledge that not all depression is a bad thing. There is what might be said to be a creative form of depression when we are grieving the loss of something we need to relinquish. In this sense the depression is signalling to us that important psychic work is being achieved in the area of letting go and moving on. It will have a different quality to it, and it will not continue in the indefinite way that other forms of depressive illness can until their meaning has been discovered and attended to. For example, when the depression is about a relentless compulsive pressure to be busy at the cost of attending to other aspects of our lives. The depression in this context might be signalling for us to stop and slow down, in order that we re-evaluate our purpose and direction in life.

Depression and pressure are linked and it is interesting that pressure forms part of the word depression, suggesting that one of the factors involved in depressive episodes is about a build-up of pressure. The task is to ascertain what the particular pressure is about. It could be regarding feelings and emotions that have had to be kept in, as a way of banishing them from conscious awareness, until even our inner unconscious reservoirs become full and the pressure builds up to dangerous levels. It also includes the pressures we put ourselves under when we drive ourselves relentlessly to attain some unrealistic standard of perfection set by our internal authority figures. DW Winnicott has a wonderful turn of phrase for this when he says, 'Perfection belongs to machines.'[55] Not surprisingly, such pressure generates huge amounts of anger which when it can't be externalised appropriately, becomes so often another contributory factor in depression. As the anger and the causes of feeling angry are heard and attended to, the person often begins to feel better in themselves. Our anger is usually a cover for other more painful feelings beneath it.

Compliant people who have spent their lives fitting in with what others want and trying to please are usually angry underneath the placid exterior and the face that smiles as they are asked to take on yet another job. Saints are often very angry people beneath all the good deeds and apparent selflessness. It is said that Mother Teresa was unable to extend the same compassionate stance to her staff as that for which she is renowned towards the poor she gave herself to unstintingly. The difficulty for those compelled to be saintly is that it is very difficult to say no. They care ceaselessly for others but cannot care also for themselves. Their whole lives hitherto have conditioned them into saying yes and not minding. So others take advantage of their not-minding and use them. They become family, community and institutional work-horses because they are renowned for not complaining – not externally anyway – though within them there is a great deal of angry protest going on. However, as yet none of this is able to be externalised and so they continue to get walked over like the proverbial doormat, angry as hell but unable to say so. It all gets buried inside them, layer upon layer of it, until one day something happens to allow the increasing depression to break through, as a symptom of the body's despair and protest at finding itself trapped in such an intolerable situation.

The endless cycle of doing good for others but endless harm to oneself: it's all become one way traffic. It can take considerable time to realise that it does not have to be that way. Doing things for others can go alongside caring for oneself, and the quality of the caring for others will improve immeasurably when our own needs are also being attended to. Otherwise caring gets tinged with resentment or worse, a vicarious needing of the other as the only way personal needs can be met. Using another to meet a need in oneself is a form of abuse, and of course when that situation occurs all concerned are the losers.

It can happen with parents who feel they need their child to stay a child in order that they can care for them, as this is the only way they feel they have of caring for themselves. This happens in various subtle ways. Covert messages are sent out every time the child does something remotely independent and therefore separate. 'Oh do be careful, are you sure you'll manage?', which immediately sows seeds of doubt about their ability to manage independently, and subtly keeps them dependent. You see this happening not just within the parent-child relationship but in any relationship where one person takes upon themselves a parental role and the other falls into a dependent stance. Nor is such a dynamic linked just to families. We have to think very carefully about our attitudes towards what are termed developing countries so that we don't foster dependence when they are making it clear they want independence, and how we negotiate that transition.

The consequence of fostering dependence to meet a need within ourselves is that every move to independence is experienced as a threat, and similarly for the dependent other, the struggle to separate gets tinged with guilt and bad feeling about becoming independent. We will all be familiar with the phrase 'tied to mother's apron strings' used to describe the 'pull' that keeps any of us tied to home and its assumed safety, rather than feeling free to go exploring, see what's out there, come to our own conclusions, and most importantly, learn that our inevitable mistakes are an important part of the learning process. M Scott Peck reflects on this capacity within us to be reluctant to cut the metaphorical apron strings in whatever sphere that dynamic expresses itself. He writes:

> We all have a sick self and a healthy self. No matter how neurotic or even psychotic we may be, even if we seem to be totally fearful and completely rigid, there is still a part of us, however small, that wants us to grow, that likes change and development, that is attracted to the new and unknown, and that is willing to do the work and take the risks in spiritual evolution. And no matter how seemingly healthy and spiritually evolved we are, there is still a part of us, however small, that does not want us to exert ourselves, that clings to the old and familiar, fearful of any change or effort, desiring comfort at any cost and absence of pain at any price, even if the penalty be ineffectiveness, stagnation, or regression. In some of us our healthy self seems pathetically small, wholly dominated by the laziness and fearfulness of our monumental sick self. Others of us may be rapidly growing, our dominant healthy self reaching eagerly upward in the struggle to evolve toward godhood; the healthy self however, must always be vigilant against the laziness of the sick self that still lurks within us. In this one respect we human beings are all equal. Within each and every one of us there are two selves, one sick and one healthy – the life urge and death urge, if you will.[56]

That passage illustrates the human dilemma and the pull between life and death that we spoke about earlier and which features in depression with its deadening affect and effect. Growing psychologically into maturity inevitably poses problems, as we are faced with the dilemmas associated with not necessarily pleasing important authority figures. Therein lies the problem. Dr Anthony Storr puts the aetiology of this state of affairs very succinctly when he writes:

> People who are liable to severe depressive reactions find difficulty in personal relations because they are ultimately looking for something which they should have had in infancy from their mothers, and which it is impossible for them to obtain in an adult relationship. Their personalities are formed upon the basis of repressing and defending themselves against the intensely hostile feelings which the scars of infantile deprivation have left. They hate those whom they love since they cannot get from them what they really need, and since they dare not show this hate for fear of losing even that which they have, they turn it inwards against themselves in self-torment and despair.[57]

It can be seen what a dilemma is posed for the person who harbours aggressive feelings linked to unmet needs at a vulnerable and dependant stage in life, with no ability to express it appropriately: the longing and hunger for love, yet the perpetual disappointment that no one can provide what was missing in those early formative years. The task of healing, very broadly speaking, is to come to terms with that profound loss, and be helped to develop a different and more compassionate relationship with ourselves and with the world, which will involve finding a more constructive way of processing aggressive feelings rather than taking them out on oneself. Of course, this propensity to turn one's aggression against oneself also becomes a prototype for the whole way in which we relate with ourselves, so that compassion gets lost in unrealistic expectations of perfectionism, to be the best or better, driving oneself further and further to achieve the longed-for hope of approval. Inevitably, because it is so unrealistic, this system is doomed to break down eventually, which in the overall scheme of things can be a creative turning point. However, it can also be experienced as very frightening bearing in mind that the whole ethos of compliant people-pleasing is to gain approval. It becomes the *modus vivendi*, and so powerful is this need that there are some who at some level prefer to remain depressed rather than risk disapproval from important others. Such is the power of our unmet needs.

Whatever the origins of this state of affairs in early life, the main source of the terror in adult life is from within the personality, as by now we have inevitably absorbed within ourselves the amassed templates of our early experiences in relation to authority figures, harbouring a host of critical and criticising elements now controlling us from within. All the while the inner dictators rule, and we remain captive to their tyranny, increasingly trapped into a world of pleasing and placating others, which is really about trying to please, and therefore silence, our inner dictator elements. The attacks of this part of the personality on our vulnerable true selves can be very cruel and sadistic. When this kind of situation is operating, it is not surprising that any of us could become profoundly depressed. Listening to our self-talk can be very revealing about the kind of relationship we have with ourselves. For most of us it is our life's task to be continually learning what it means to love ourselves, as we recognise the harsh standards that we would never demand of others yet exact upon ourselves.

Modifying the pressures and demands of this part of the personality is a key element in the psychotherapy of the soul. However, there will likely be huge internal resistance from what Scott Peck described as our sick self towards the healthy part of us that is wanting to get healthier. I cannot overestimate how hard standing up to these elements within the personality can be, which of course is its function – to terrify us back into subservience and submission. It is the same dynamic that operates in dictator states, where control of the people is the order of the day. And where there is control, there is fear. Fear of reprisals, which is exactly what the depressed person feels in standing up to the inner dictators by doing what they would like to do rather than what they feel they ought to do.

For someone under the shadow of inner menacing figures, the world is ruled by 'oughts' and 'shoulds', which doesn't leave much space for freedom just to be yourself. They feel continuously controlled by an inner expectation of what they ought to be, rather than an enjoyment of what they are. People caught in this trap of unrealistic expectations often reach a point when they no longer know what they think. In other words, all individuality is sacrificed to a bland compliance. They can no longer make decisions, and when asked what they might like or want, reply with the standard response 'I don't mind'. That is safe and doesn't risk upsetting anyone. They have become experts in fitting in, becoming almost invisible. They do mind of course. They mind very much, except that by now it has all become so unconscious that as part of their developed psychic economy to help them cope, they try to convince themselves that they don't mind. For a time this strategy works and they get away with it, but sooner or later the truth manifests itself and the ensuing depression is one of the signals the body has to alert its owner that all is not well. The surface may appear calm as a millpond, that being the image that they present to the world. However, underneath this calm, placid, uncomplaining persona is a veritable storm of swirling emotional currents that breaks through every now and then in apparently uncharacteristic outbursts of anger. In its most extreme form it is the violent act committed by someone of whom the shocked neighbours say 'but he/she was so gentle, they would never hurt anyone'. Anthony Storr makes an interesting comment linked with this when he writes:

> At the opposite pole to such a breeding ground for violence are those middle-class households, often professional Christians in which aggression is so much taboo that a cross word or a momentary loss of temper is regarded as a crime. Such a milieu not infrequently produces children who are quite unable to stand up for themselves or even compete adequately with their peers.[58]

We see the two ends of the spectrum, rather than an integrated ability to deal with aggressive feelings. It is this suppression of aggressive feelings that is likely to be a factor in encouraging aggressive feelings to find expression passively.

Passive aggression could be thought of as the hidden face of anger. Such people present as gentle, tame souls that wouldn't hurt a fly, so their anger finds other ways out, a bit like an underground stream trickling out here and there – unless something happens to unleash the dammed-up emotion, in which case you will be faced with a raging torrent that envelops everything in its path. Sudden bereavement can have this effect, or some other catastrophic event that completely disarms the person's defence system, allowing all manner of things to emerge. This is upsetting for the owner and others alike. 'This isn't me at all!' they cry. It is true that what is emerging isn't the image of themselves that they or anyone else has known. However, for the discerning and those sufficiently sensitive, the warning signs have been there for all to see – the passivity and slowness that causes everyone around them to feel intensely annoyed and irritable while they themselves appear blissfully unruffled and unaware of the impact they have.

In the context of what we have been saying, the person who is passively angry cannot bear to be in connection with that emotion in themselves, possibly because they were never allowed to in their formative years, and so distances themself from it by putting it into those around them. That way they remain calm and everyone else gets wound up. So for example, they may perpetually arrive late and derive vicarious satisfaction from keeping people waiting. It also facilitates the grand entrance and the skilled apology which ensures they are noticed. It is likely that somewhere in their earlier experience they have felt profoundly unnoticed and ignored, which has caused very painful wounds that generate deep hurt and much corresponding anger. Inside they long to feel acknowledged, which is the birthright of us all. Yet the reaction they generate around them is one of irritation which further alienates them from the emotional contact and acknowledgement they crave but cannot communicate in more satisfactory, and therefore satisfying, ways.

Passive aggressors often express their aggression through being very slow and tardy, which also has the effect of irritating the people around them. I am sure we can all think of occasions when we have felt irritated by the length of time a seemingly simple task is taken to accomplish. And equally the times we ourselves have fallen prey to this mechanism as a covert way of expressing protest. The toddler in us is still very capable of dawdling, especially when we don't want to do a particular task.

Withholding is another face of anger. The giveaway is the effect that people unconsciously using this form of anger generate around them, as we have already begun to see in the previous paragraph. There is a lovely example of this in Virginia Axline's therapeutic journey with Dibs, a young emotionally troubled boy who initially would not talk or play but who through lovingly reliable and consistent therapeutic help was able to re-find himself. She writes of a dialogue with Dibs,

> 'Papa says people just talk to people,' Dibs said. There was a twinkle in his eyes. 'Papa says I ought to talk to him, but I don't. I listen to him, but I don't talk to him. No, often I do not answer him. It upsets him very much.'

Talking had become an issue between the two of them and Dibs was an expert at withholding speech as a way of getting back at his critical father.[59]

Withholding is often expressed in the sexual arena. One party may be angry with their partner, or may be carrying a residue of anger from a previous relationship, that gets superimposed on the current relationship, in the way that intimate relationships do become a repository for unfinished business from the past. Such unexpressed and unresolved anger can very often find an outlet through withholding sexually, with all the repercussions that can ensue.

Other examples of withholding as a means of displacing anger are the occasions when we agree to do a task which we don't really want to do but feel unable in the circumstances to say no. The resentment in such a situation gets expressed in putting off the task, in forgetting it, in needing numerous reminders, all of which serve only to further irritate everybody involved. At the same time, when an opportunity is offered not to do it, we may decline and manage to very convincingly reaffirm our willingness to do the task, illustrating that the difficulty is really within ourselves in the form of our inner authority figures whom as yet we have not learned to stand up to. The cycle goes round again, leaving others increasingly frustrated and annoyed. Withholding exerts huge control and arouses intense frustration in others. It has to be asked, whose fury is getting expressed? The tragedy of such covert expressions of anger is that no creative resolution can take place, because the feeling has been displaced from its original source. Once the feeling is back where it belongs and able to be thought about and understood, then the potential for dealing with it more satisfactorily is available.

Intellectually one may know very well that a clear 'No, I don't want to do this' would simplify life for all concerned, but of course that is the very thing that poses such a difficulty. I imagine we can all, in varying degrees, identify with the difficulties involved in saying no which lie behind this distorted way of expressing anger, anger not just at the circumstance for creating this pressure, but anger with ourselves at our difficulty in saying no. Getting cross with oneself never did anybody any good.

Displacement of our anger onto someone or something else is a common mechanism. Only recently I realised how I had snapped forcefully at my husband for a remark he made; my anger was actually much more to do with someone else who had been making similar remarks but towards whom I wasn't able to be angry. As a result it got displaced. Partners and friends in close relationships are sitting ducks for the displacement of angry feelings. Someone has a bad day at the office, keeps their feelings under control, and then a small annoyance at home can unleash more than the incident warrants.

Self-harming behaviour is another face of anger associated with an inability to externalise angry feelings safely and appropriately, manifesting itself in a variety of ways, for example when a person feels compelled to cut, starve, or damage themselves. Dawn Collins, in a paper on this subject, writes,

> Self harm is about communication. It is like a scream without a sound: painful, distraught, frightening and perplexing. My hypothesis is that self injury is a symptom. This symptom may take the place of words, and functions as a means of communication.[60]

A theme which psychotherapist Maggie Turp endorses is this: 'The therapist's work is to provide a place where what has previously only been able to be shown, can start to be told, narrated in words.'[61]

It is outside the purpose of this book to consider this subject in too much detail, wanting really to acknowledge it as a particular face of anger. However, it feels important that we also recognise the less acknowledged forms of self harm that we all get caught up in from time to time. What about doing too much, or giving ourselves a hard time when we haven't lived up to the perfectionist ideal? Beating ourselves up metaphorically for some perceived or actual failure? Reckless driving, over-eating or inappropriate eating habits that deplete us rather than nourish us, damage to our health through persistently inadequate sleep? Refusal to seek medical attention for fear of what might be diagnosed or discovered? We all know how destructive these forms of attack on ourselves can be, and it may be salutary to reflect on what our purpose in engaging in these behaviours is about.

It also seems to me that into this category of self-harm we need to think about the masochistic muttering that attempts to pass as thinking. It attempts to resolve, but actually just keeps the whole angry internal dialogue going, in a kind of circular mental activity. I have heard it referred to as 'mentating', whilst the psychoanalyst Betty Joseph refers to it as 'chuntering'. Either way, it is a form of pseudo-thinking that achieves nothing except to further fan the fires of our anger and exhaust us in the process. It uses up a lot of time, spoiling time that could have been used more profitably and enjoyably, yet has a particularly seductive pull about it, and in that sense has a kind of addictive quality. It can be a very difficult habit to relinquish, because it has become part of our defensive armoury and coping strategy. Despite its self-destructive quality, it gives the illusion that one is attending to distress, and that by engaging with it in this way, relief will be found. In fact it magnifies the distress by keeping it going, even if for a short time, as with alcohol and drugs, there is some relief. It is the longing for relief, that forms such a strong pull, though paradoxically, rather than offering relief, it serves only to keep us in the quagmire of despair. What John Bunyan in his *Pilgrim's Progress* might have been referring to when he wrote about Christian's pilgrimage which took him to the Slough of Despond. There is something particularly tenacious about this face of anger, that wants to pull us down and keep us in the quagmire. If one feels oneself to be wading through thick mud that sticks, it is hard to feel free to enjoy life. I quote from a paper given by Betty Joseph, which illustrates this issue. She writes:

> There is a very malignant type of self-destructiveness... which is I think in the nature of an addiction – an addiction to near-death... Such patients feel in thrall to a part of the self that dominates and imprisons them and will not let them escape, even though they see life beckoning outside.
>
> I am discussing here that it is not only that he is dominated by an aggressive part of himself, which attempts to control and destroy, but that this part is actively sadistic towards another part of the self which is masochistically caught up in this process and that this has become an addiction. This process has always I believe, an internal counterpart, and in patients really dedicated to self-destructiveness, this internal situation has a very strong hold over their thinking, and their quiet moments, their capacity for mulling things over or the lack of it. The kind of thing one sees is

this. These patients pick up very readily something that has been going on in their minds or in an external relationship and start to use it over and over again in some circular type of mental activity in which they get completely caught up, so that they go over and over with very little variation the same actual or anticipated issue. This mental activity, which I think is best described by the word 'chuntering' is very important. The *Oxford English Dictionary* (1979) describes chuntering as 'mutter, murmur, grumble, find fault, complain'.[62]

As with anything to which we feel in some way addicted to, we need to understand its purpose and what function it serves before there can be any hope of relinquishing it. The early parts of all of us developed ways of being which served us usefully at a time in our lives when we were helplessly dependant upon our caregivers, and this particular way of dealing with early distress is a kind of withdrawal from a helpful and therefore satisfying relationship with the other, to a withdrawal into oneself with one part of oneself turning against another part. With a civil war going on within us, it's not difficult to see how our thinking can get warped and further this destructive state of affairs. It generates a sense of desperation and hopelessness, which can then escalate ultimately into thoughts of suicide and wanting to end it all. The question that needs to be asked is, what is it they are wanting to end? I suggest in this context it might well be this awful self-destructiveness that keeps them stuck in the mire of despair.

Suicide can be a statement about many things, one of which is the ultimate despairing face of anger that has reached the end of the road. The anger that cannot get through to the other, that wants to make a final statement to the world, to say 'see what you have made me do', a despair and rage that makes one feel there can be no other way to end intolerable distress. The unspoken message is very often 'what do I have to do to be heard?' Suicide takes many forms, but whatever the form, angry protest is tied up in such a desperate action. Dawn Collins, in describing her work with a particular suicidal patient who had taken an overdose, tells of the significant turning point when feelings could be put into words, thus reducing the need to find relief in cutting herself. She writes:

> Over time, the cutting became less frequent. Words began to replace the act, and she began to experience a relief at her new ability to articulate her terrified and abandoned feelings.
>
> The overlap between self-injury and the wish to die is blurred. While there is a profoundly different motivation operating when the prime wish is to damage the body, rather than to die, the risk of suicide must be taken seriously.[63]

There are the suicide attempts where the hope is that they will be found, or they themselves call someone and usually evoke a response. There are those that are determined to end it all and do. Often the real sources of such hurt go back much further than the immediate circumstances, but often it is the current situation that bears the brunt of their fury. Suicide is an expression of unrelieved and unremitting anger from untold hurt that, because it hasn't been able to be shared, feeds an endless despair and leads the tormented sufferer to want to end it all. It has to be asked; what is it they are wanting to end? What has become so intolerable that they cannot bear it any longer? Is it their external situation or the suffering inside them, or a combination of both? These are questions which can only find an appropriate answer from within the person in such distress.

This picks up a theme we have returned to several times, about choices, and whether when faced with a personal crisis we choose the path of self-destruction or the path that is ultimately more life-enhancing. I am told that the Chinese meaning of the word 'crisis' is both danger, but also opportunity. Perhaps the danger is that we might miss the opportunity for growth that a crisis presents us with. Suicidal thoughts are a potential crisis, but another way of looking at the crisis is that it alerts us to the necessity to change. Perhaps a particular way of being has to end, rather than life itself, in which case the crisis becomes life-promoting in helping us start the process of rebuilding life in ways we want. Our next chapter is about using anger creatively, so that it works for us rather than in the destructive ways that militate against our best interests, which this chapter has focussed on.

## NOTES

[42] M Scott Peck, *The Road Less Travelled*, Hutchinson and Co., 1978, 1983, p.266, Arrow Books, 1990

[43] Robin Skynner, *Explorations with Families; Group Analysis and Family Therapy*, Tavistock/Routledge, 1987, p.152

[44] M Scott Peck, *People of the Lie*, Arrow, 1990, p.138

[45] Joseph Sandler, *Projection, Identification, Projective Identification*, Karnac Books Ltd, London, p.145

[46] Thomas H Ogden: *Projective Identification and Psychotherapeutic technique*, Jason Aronson Inc, 1982, p.129, republished with permission by Karnac Books Ltd, 1992

[47] Neville Symington, *The Analytic Experience*, Free Association Books Ltd, 1986, p.22

[48] Maggie Scarf, *Intimate Partners*, Century Paperbacks, 1987, p.313

[49] Genesis 1

[50] Neville Symington, *The Analytic Experience: Lectures from the Tavistock*, Free Association Books Ltd, 1986, p.271

[51] Mathew 7:7

[52] Luke 17:21

[53] Mathew 7:14

[54] Mathew 6:20

[55] DW Winnicott, *Playing and Reality*, Tavistock publications, 1971, p.139

[56] M Scott Peck, *The Road Less travelled*, Hutchinson and Co., 1978, and 1983, pp.295/6, with subsequent reprints by Arrow Books, 1990

[57] Anthony Storr, *Human Aggression*, The Penguin Press, London, 1968, p.80

[58] Anthony Storr, *Human Aggression*, The Penguin Press, London, 1968, p.61

[59] Virginia M Axline, *Dibs in Search of Self*, Penguin Books, 1964, p.138

[60] Dawn Collins, 'Attacks on the Body', taken from her paper in *Psychodynamic Counselling*, Routledge, November, 1996, p.463

[61] Maggie Turp, quoted from a report in the *Counselling and Psychotherapy Journal*, June, 2000, p.7

[62] Betty Joseph, 'Addiction to Near Death', taken from a paper originally presented to a scientific meeting of the British Psycho-Analytical Society, 20 May 1981, and was first published in 1982 in the *International Journal of Psycho-Analysis*, 63:449–56, Routledge, and currently taken from *Psychic Equilibrium and Psychic Change: Selected Papers of Betty Joseph*, edited by Michael Feldman and Elizabeth Bott Spillus, 1989

[63] Dawn Collins, 'Attacks on the Body', taken from her paper in *Psychodynamic Counselling*, Routledge, November, 1996, p.469

## Creative Anger

What do we mean by creative anger? It feels important for us to acknowledge that anger is energy. We only have to witness a screaming infant or a toddler in a tantrum, or recall some of our own angry experiences to know how much energy is tied up in the angry response. We have either heard said, or expressed the sentiment ourselves over a particular situation, 'it makes my blood boil', illustrating the energy involved in anger. We speak of becoming 'hot and bothered', of 'losing our cool', or being like a 'raging furnace' or a 'roaring tornado'. These images convey immense and powerful energy. This is the kind of energy that is available to us to use in a way that can make a difference to bring about the necessary changes we want in our lives. It is also the amount of potentially life-giving energy that is suppressed when we are afraid of using our anger creatively. It doesn't take an Einstein to realise we are the losers when we quite literally bury that amount of energy.

In addition to not having it available to use as part of our personal bank of resources, it requires a great deal of energy to keep it buried and out of service. Not surprisingly, people who are deeply angry but unable to access it are often chronically tired. The theme tune 'I'm so tired' might well be a substitute for 'I'm so angry', angry about having to be so busy to justify primarily to ourselves our existence upon this earth; angry about the strain of feeling we have the burden of the world on our shoulders – who wouldn't feel tired carrying that degree of responsibility and feeling no possibility of being able to put that burden down? Angry perhaps that in every and all situations it feels as if we end up doing all the work. It's all down to us to keep relationships alive, unless we do something, nothing will happen. The world depends on us – or so it can sometimes feel. These give just a flavour of the kind of situations that generate deep and pervasive anger which can seep into every muscle and cell of our bodies –

unless, that is, we are able to find a more creative way of discharging and utilising the current that anger generates.

So how can we use our anger creatively, and what do we mean by creative anger? In a very basic kind of way we need to be asking, is a particular way of responding helpful or could it be potentially helpful, to the current situation? It very much picks up on a recurring theme in this book concerning whether a particular activity is life-enhancing or death-dealing. My understanding of the word *creative* is of something that has energy and life, and holds huge potential to facilitate something that could make a difference to the quality of our lives and the situations we find ourselves in. In other words, it opens up the possibility for something new to emerge, a different way of responding perhaps, which could facilitate a different outcome. The examples mentioned earlier all had fairly destructive connotations – tornados for example, whip things up leaving a trail of destruction in their wake. A roaring furnace is something full of heat that burns things up and destroys everything in its vicinity. However, both those examples although they might initially be very destructive, can ultimately facilitate a new beginning. Things have to be rebuilt which implies starting all over again, allowing for them to be done differently. This is an important concept for us to hold on to, that even apparent destruction and destructiveness can, in the overall scheme of things, prove to facilitate something very creative. David Attenborough, writing of his observations about plants, draws on this theme when writing about the creative aspect of extensive fires in Australia, for example.

> Flowering is also greatly influenced by previous fires. Chemical substances in the smoke produced by the fire impregnate the surface layers of the soil. When, perhaps months later, rain does fall, it dissolves these chemicals and washes them down more deeply into the ground where they reach the dormant seeds. It is these substances that are the essential triggers for germination... As a result of this discovery, botanical gardens all over the world are now able to germinate seeds that until recently had resisted all attempts to coax them into life. They are put into tents and smoke puffed over them.[64]

In this business of creativity everything has the potential to be creative if one has the patience and belief to see something through to its ultimate conclusions. Fire in biblical writing is a popular symbol of purification and cleansing, paving the way for a new beginning. So what might initially seem destructive can, if we are willing, hold potential for creativity to emerge. We need to hold in mind the larger picture – while fire is raging it seems to burn up everything in its path, but as David Attenborough commented, the smoke actually releases triggers in the soil that facilitate germination in plants which had 'until recently resisted all attempts to coax them into life'. And of course I am aware that fire when it goes out of control is extremely dangerous and frightening, whereas the kind of fire that generates intense heat within a furnace is contained heat and therefore can be managed safely. It is not without significance that the containment of a furnace in an industrial setting is the catalyst for transformation. The same analogy can apply to feeling states that have the quality of a raging furnace when it is contained and able to be used creatively. Think of how chemicals react when they are heated, and how out of the resulting mixture a new substance is produced. Or what about precious stones, many of which are formed deeply underground as a result of intense heat and pressure? Diamonds are one such example. The point I am making is that something very precious and beautiful can emerge out of sustained heat and pressure when there is the resolve to dig deep and discover it. Our anger can, in a different context, serve as the catalyst to bring about change in a way that allows for something very precious and lasting to be discovered. It gives us the drive and the energy to pursue the kind of changes we are wanting, either within ourselves or in our circumstance. The two are usually linked in some way.

I wonder what other metaphors come to mind to help us in our explorations around this theme of creative anger. What immediately comes to my mind is the description used of someone who gets things moving after a time when it has seemed the situation is stuck. We describe such a person as being, in that context, like dynamite. Yes, it is true, as we have just been thinking, that dynamite has the potential to blow things up and destroy, but carefully used it has enormous potential to be creative. It is what we do with it and how we use it that defines whether dynamite is creative or destructive. Indeed, dynamite is resorted to when it seems there is no other way through an impasse, and carefully and skilfully used it does make a difference. It can change a landscape forever, as for example when new roads are made through mountains, linking two hitherto unconnected areas together, with all the potential for better communication facilitated by that connection. That is the kind of difference I am thinking of when I think of anger being creative. It is our appropriately expressed anger that makes the way for better communication with others. When we react, it could be said the feeling has us in its grip and we feel at its mercy in a rather unhelpful way, or so it feels at the time. However, when we can separate from it enough through having thought about it and understood its aetiology, we are then in a better position to respond, rather than react. We then have the feeling, rather than the feeling having us. When it has us, we can end up saying or doing things we might later regret. This may sound like semantics, but in reality can make the difference between being creative or destructive. If we have the feeling, rather than the feeling having us, we then have it within us as a resource to use. Our anger has become a creative tool that can facilitate better, more open communication – whether that be with partners, spouses, children or other members of our particular family. The ramifications are endless, stretching out into the work environment, on to the international scene between communities and countries, or, much nearer to home, improving the communication within ourselves. That is the area we need to address first, for it is our capacity to be in better communication with ourselves that paves the way for better communications in the world around us.

It may be that you are wondering what I mean by such a statement, particularly as some who are especially terrified of anger (both their own, and consequently anger in others) have long since learnt to deny that they are even angry. It could be said they are out of communication with that aspect of themselves. These are placid souls, who wouldn't harm a flea, we are told, yet who quite suddenly and unexpectedly commit atrocities that leave those closest to them reeling in shock; an illustration of what can happen when a feeling has us, rather than us having the feeling and being in charge of it. The energy of their anger has been damned up for too long – ultimately something seemingly insignificant serves as the trigger for the dam to break, and then it feels as if all hell is let loose.

Of course I think very often the fear that all hell will break loose is often greater than the reality, and can become a synonym for the fear of reprisals if we dare to be angry. As I write I find myself recalling the amusing (in retrospect) incident of a nun whom, whilst a novice in the novitiate of a particular religious community, first of all discovering that such emotions resided within her, and then having her first experience of being able to externalise her anger, and the terror experienced by that part of her for having done so. Not surprisingly, having for so long kept such feelings under lock and key, when initially they emerged the outcome surprised her more than those around her, whose reactions she had feared but who in the event seemed to rather enjoy this new development within her. She writes:

> Despite all the pain, there was a steady healing going on, of the memories and of the body. Trust was built up, and though it was very fragile at first, I could actually believe myself loved not after I had ceased to be a failure but while I was still a dismal one, while I was apparently useless and weak... for at that point I was still hobbling around on crutches.
>
> There was still a further test. Could I be angry, even express that anger, and still feel accepted? Of course, I hadn't articulated this question even to myself. But I realised now that there was a great inner need for assurance on that one. In my evangelical upbringing the emphasis had been on restraint. 'The fruit of the Spirit is... self-control' had been taught almost to the exclusion of that other fruit meekness, which is really knowing how to be angry at the right time, in the right way and for the right reasons. I had certainly not been used to angry outbursts at home.
>
> Then one day it happened. I was working in the pantry at the time, and on that evening it seemed that the stream of sisters storming in to complain about this and grumble about that had been more steady and more bitter than usual. The 'oughts' and

'musts' flew at me from all directions, doubtless much of it deserved. But the pantry was also a useful and central place where people could, and often did, vent their feelings, whether or not it was directly the pantry sister's affair.

Each sister charged in more wrathful than the one before, each one shattering my nerves just a bit more. Finally, driven beyond endurance, I fled to the refectory to wash down the tables. But inwardly I was so furious, it all exploded. Picking up a rather revolting dishcloth, I hurled it the full length of the refectory with a throw that would have earned me a round of applause in my former cricketing days.

'If that's community life,' I shouted at the top of my voice (in the middle of what is a silent place), 'you can stick it on the wall where it belongs.'

Silence. Then slowly the door opened; a face appeared round it. It was one of the younger sisters. She showed no surprise – certainly no shock. She took in the situation. Just a novice having the atmospherics, her face seemed to say, and she withdrew without a word.

Later when I went to apologise, she laughed about it so uproariously with me that I knew she had actually rather enjoyed the moment. At any rate she fully accepted the anger as normal. That was a revelation to me.

One outburst was not enough to bring total conviction of course. Nor was it sufficient simply to know when other novices became angry, they weren't shown the door. I had to know that I wouldn't either.

The next occasion when I erupted was, as it happens, very justifiable. A sister had been outrageously interfering in the department for which I was responsible at the time. She wouldn't have dared taken such liberties with a more senior sister. Even so, she must have been wholly unprepared for the vehemence of my explosion. Sadly, I seem to be far more articulate when I am angry than at normal times. The words poured forth like lava from a volcano. When eventually I stopped, I went as white as a sheet and fled outside, where I stood by a row of dustbins trembling all over.

'That's that,' I thought. 'All these years of training and the pain I've been through... it's all over in four minutes flat.' And I seriously believed that once my misconduct had been reported I should be asked to pack my bags and go.

Imagine my amazement, therefore, when not only was I not required to leave, but the response from my superior was, 'Thank God. You are actually learning to be angry at last.'[65]

What comes through from that experience is the maturity of the community who looked upon anger as normal, and even expressed relief that it was at last able to find expression. There was also a sense of understanding that sometimes our anger doesn't come out all neatly packaged, and I think it is the fear of making a mess that can add impetus to denying anger in circles where control is all important. The greater the need for self-control, the greater the need to keep everything under wraps, until everything feels so stuck the very relationship feels strangled.

I recall an experience many years ago in a gathering of Christian people meeting together in someone's home, of one particular lady informing us with great conviction that she was in her sixth decade and had never been angry in her life. This was said with complete sincerity and clearly felt to be a virtue. It was not my place to make any comment in that setting or context, but I was privately aware how angry she was by how much anger she generated in me and, I might add, in her husband who she complained was always flying off the handle. It would seem she unconsciously projected it all into him, and he, poor man, was carrying a double dose – hers as well as his. I don't wonder he raged. She was an ardent and devout church-goer, which he had been but significantly, he now refused to attend, which was perhaps his form of protest. Neither it seems could, at that time, resolve their conflicts in a more creative way, with the result that it got acted out between them in a destructive kind of way, keeping them stuck in their entrenched positions, with him being seen as difficult and her feeling virtuous. It may have been that if she could allow herself to be in communication with her own angry feelings, that he might have become less difficult. As it was, the situation felt very stuck and, to outward appearances at any rate, they seemed to tolerate each other, rather than enjoy each other.

So what is meant by being in better communication with ourselves? My understanding of this concept is about listening to ourselves and gradually and increasingly being in greater harmony with all the different and disparate parts of ourselves. The angry child is the hurt child who feels unheard, who feels no-one can be bothered to attend to their distress, who feels in some way dismissed, a nuisance for having any needs, and whilst that child may learn to manage by keeping it all in, sooner or later those feelings will have to be attended to. Ultimately it is the adult part of all of us that needs to attend to the earlier child parts of ourselves, not aggressively or impatiently but with compassion and acceptance. I heard it once said by the psychotherapist Janet Lake at a workshop on Anger in Norwich, 'that the greatest betrayal is the betrayal of ourselves, by ourselves'. I found that a profound statement which I have never forgotten. We betray ourselves when we deny ourselves the opportunity to feel what we feel. As we have said before, feelings in themselves are neither right or wrong. It is what we do with them that becomes a moral issue, and to shut off whole areas of ourselves and thus restrict both what we can emotionally receive from others, as well as give out to others, seems to me much more immoral than the honest expression of what we might be feeling. We could be likened to a radio station – the better the reception, the wider the range of frequency that can be picked up, and therefore the more useful and valuable is our radio. The very fact that we so often speak about 'the vibes' indicates that we are already familiar with the continual interplay of psychic transmissions, and the giving and receiving of messages that goes on all the time in any relationship.

Feelings that are heard have the potential to be resolved, not least by the fact that we develop a different relationship to them through accepting them as a valid part of ourselves. The acceptance of anything that is a part of us, rather than wanting to banish it, is bound to affect how we feel about ourselves. It is likely to mean we will feel less terrified and anxious about their existence, and can eventually feel that we and our feelings can reside together reasonably harmoniously in the same body. Only recently a particular patient who has re-found her health after a long and debilitating depression said to me when we reflected upon the factors that had helped her to re-find herself, 'I am less afraid of my feelings.' With that profound development she has been able to gain confidence in managing herself and her feelings.

For all of us, when certain parts of ourselves have less power to frighten and intimidate us, the outcome is necessarily a state of better well-being. In the light of what I was saying earlier, it could be said that we have the feeling, rather than the feeling having us. Those elements no longer have to be banished and located in others, or in certain parts of our bodies.

'Wholeness' is a popular word in some communities. We need to grasp that being a whole person is not some idealised and mythical state of having arrived, (as I once thought) but something rather more gutsy and earthy, whereby there is a comfortable acceptance of a wide range of feeling states to which we can with genuineness say 'this is me, this is how I feel at this moment' rather than the constricted range allowable when we are under the constraints of the 'oughts' and 'shoulds'. This achievement is likely to be a lifetime's task, as of course we all have different emotional areas that are for us our Achilles heel and with which we have to do business with on a regular basis. It's like having a toolbox with a variety of tools for different tasks, some of which we feel more comfortable and at ease in using than others which need us to learn how to use them. Anger very often falls into that category of 'others' and is a tool which we may well need help in learning how to handle and use, so that as William Blake makes clear in his poem A Poison Tree, it becomes a friend rather than a foe. He writes:

> I was angry with my friend.
> I told my wrath, my wrath did end.
> I was angry with my foe.
> I told it not, my wrath did grow.
>
> And I water'd it in fears,
> Night and morning with my tears.
> And I sunned it with smiles.
> And with soft deceitful smiles.
> And it grew both day and night,
> Till it bore an apple bright.
> And my foe beheld it shine
> And he knew that it was mine.

> And into my garden stole,
> When the night had veiled the pole,
> In the morning glad I see,
> My foe stretched out beneath the tree.[66]

It is significant that denied anger accumulates fear and 'deceitful wiles', as we cover over our resentful feelings with smiles. It is also salutary that however much we might try to turn it into 'an apple bright', our foe is not fooled and ultimately in the context of the poem, it killed the relationship. It is a true friend with whom we feel safe enough to express our anger when necessary and know that it will be respected and in all likelihood deepen the friendship rather than destroy it. Paradoxically, it is when we are deceitful with out nearest and dearest that something gets lost in the relationship.

Remembering that anger and energy are linked, it can often be that our angry feelings can be the stimulus to change, so that for example where perhaps previously we felt unable to say no to anyone and got increasingly put upon and taken for granted, it may be that we begin to reflect on this state of affairs, and can consider why it is that we find saying no so difficult. It may then be that a moment of insight reveals to us why this might be so, and with that realisation may come the strength to respond to a particular situation differently, in ways that hopefully serve us better. That is what I mean by creative anger. It has been the catalyst to facilitate something new and life-giving to emerge, as we learn to attend to undeveloped aspects of ourselves and make space for inner growth. By attending to ourselves, I do not mean a passive licking of our wounds in an endless 'poor me' session, but rather something much more vigorous that allows for something creative to emerge from the difficulty, which will be different to its antecedents, when perhaps there was a sense of resigned impotence. How often do we hear the cry, and express it ourselves, 'what's the point of saying anything, it won't make any difference?' Maybe not, or not immediately, though I venture to suggest that when we learn to speak with conviction and clarity it will make a difference. For a start we will feel different for having externalised what we feel, and the other party will, at the very least, have heard what has been said, even if for the time being they choose to ignore it. Rome wasn't built in a day, and changing any system takes time. The child part of all of us has sometimes to be reminded that tomorrow is another day and there will be other opportunities to try to resolve whatever is bothering us, even if the early part of us tries hard sometimes to suggest otherwise. Some of us carry anxious infants that need much soothing and reassurance.

Creativity implies growth and growth needs space. But like bulbs that flower in spring, there is a necessary prelude to the visible signs of growth, when important changes are taking place beneath the surface. As Sister Margaret Magdalen reminds us,

> Bewildering as it all seems at the time, it is actually in the darkness that most of our growing is done. The rule in the natural world – growth in the darkness of the soil, growth in the darkness of the womb, applies to the spiritual too.[67]

This is why it is important that we do attend to our feelings, and particularly those emotions that rumble beneath the surface, affecting us in powerful even if apparently less obvious ways. Just as the keel and hull of a ship, for the most part submerged beneath the waterline and therefore unseen, is crucial for the ship's stability and capacity to re-centre when tossed in rough seas, so the activities that go on within us at a subliminal level have a huge impact on our capacity to function creatively in all weathers.

In a very real sense it is the structure of the hull which dictates the size of ship that can be carried, and the amount of cargo it can safely hold. Many of us it seems lose sight of that principle, and carry huge emotional cargoes that get added to every time we bury our feelings rather than attend to them. It is not difficult to see that allowing that situation to continue unmonitored leaves us very vulnerable to emotional shipwreck. This is not to say that at times of internal turbulence, when significant shifts are happening within us as we change in some deeply important way, that we don't feel as if we are sinking and about to disintegrate altogether. The difference is that with a sound hull, which if you like is synonymous with the adult, conscious part of our minds, we can integrate and therefore use past experiences to inform present ones. We are more equipped to ride the waves so to speak, and become re-centred when the storm has been negotiated. That is the function of a good keel. Indeed we say of someone who is well balanced, that they are on an even keel. The feared collapse and disintegration is of course about something that has already happened very much earlier in our lives, but resonates every time something in the current situation triggers off feeling memories associated with those early experiences. Being able to make that distinction is important in weathering the emotional storms that are a normal part of life, just as storms on the ocean are a natural feature of sea journeys. If we have belief in the vessel we are journeying in, the stormy experiences are more bearable and less terrifying. We know the ship will hold. That is very important when any of us are negotiating a crisis.

Creativity, we have said, implies growth. It is also about an openness for change. The two go together, which is fairly obvious when one thinks about it, but we sometimes need to remind ourselves of this truth, when the process is happening in us and around us. Change can be very unsettling, disturbing as it does the status quo of what we have become used to and therefore familiar with. It can feel particularly unsettling when, as often happens, it takes us into uncharted waters. I say unsettling, which is an understatement for what at times may feel terrifying! After all, this kind of journey has no guarantees, no directive map that says comfortably 'Yes, you are on the right path'. But what any of us does have is that inner light that beckons, and the inner conviction that confirms the particular path that each of us has to find and continue along. It is the development of our inner capacities that dictates how creative or otherwise our emotional responses to situations will be.

But in order for change in some form or other to occur, there has to be movement. The energy involved in creative processes has to be directed somewhere, which means in the context of our anger that the energy tied up in it needs to be used and channelled appropriately. It has to go somewhere and do something. The wellsprings of life reside in all of us, not just the chosen few, and if we can harness this source of energy, it can flow wherever it is directed and bring life in its path. Block the outflow and sooner or later there will be trouble. At the very least the subsequent build up of pressure will have its own impact. There is also the danger that in addition to very likely making us ill, if the pressure builds up too much it may eventually explode, potentially causing a terrible sense of fragmentation and disintegration. Something of this terrible sense of falling apart takes rather longer to attend to and mend than if we can release the pressures in a more contained, safe way. The unexpected outburst in the scenario of the person of whom it was said 'would never hurt a flea' yet who carried out a vicious attack that shocked his nearest and dearest, is a telling example of what can happen when the pressure builds up to intolerable proportions. How much better for all concerned that we harness the energy that our anger holds and channel it appropriately to the areas that need attending to. It is often the apparently uncharacteristic outburst that can signal to us that something within us needs attending to.

This all sounds reasonably sensible and logical, but in order for this to happen we have to understand and remove the blocks in whatever form they take, and that can be a lifelong task. If something is blocking this creative potential within us it is in our own interests and the corporate interests of the society we live in to begin to liberate ourselves, in order that all that energy is available and accessible for the task of living rather than existing. In this context it can be very salutary to begin to realise how strong can be the pull to keep ourselves diminished in some way and therefore in that sense experience something of the tenacity and strength of the death instinct as opposed to the life instinct. These are emotional currents present in varying degrees within everyone, and it may only be when we start to unravel our own particular predilections that our eyes are opened to seeing just how much at times we get caught up in the struggle between life and death. It is no wonder to me that the themes of death and resurrection are so central to the Christian religion. Our task is to relate the symbolism of those themes to the context of our own lives and the ways, perhaps unwittingly, we either keep ourselves in a state of suspended crucifixion, by what can become an addiction to suffering and pain, or we metaphorically keep ourselves stuck in the tomb, caught between the traumas of crucifixion and all it represents of our woundedness, alongside the demands of resurrection and new life, with all that they represent of challenges and risks.

The tomb can mean many different things to us at different times in our lives, and I hasten to add that following deep trauma, a protected place to recover might well be necessary – for a period. The issue for any of us is whether we are able to move out from that place and re-find life, with all the stresses and demands, uncertainties and challenges that life might imply, but also the sheer joy of feeling so fully alive; or whether we stay entombed suspended between life and death in a state of feeling half-alive. It can be very hard to move out from the particular way of being that serves to keep us entombed and it may be that we will need someone to roll away the stone, as the angel did for Jesus in the Gospel story; 'Suddenly there was a violent earthquake; an angel of the Lord came down from heaven, rolled away the stone and sat on it.'[68] It always amuses me that we are given that extra detail at the end about how the angel sat on the stone! Perhaps this was to ensure that it didn't roll back, for any who have walked this way will know that the temptation to roll back into old ways of being can be very strong at times. The biblical story of the exodus from Egypt illustrates this point very graphically. Time and again, when things got tough, they yearned for the 'melons and cucumbers of Egypt', forgetting in the stress of the moment the bondage to cruel dictators from which they were in the process of being delivered. The symbolism of the resurrection story has a great deal to say to us within the context of the struggle between life and death and the pull between creative and destructive forces within us, which I hasten to add is part of the human condition. I also think it is not without significance that all four gospel accounts record this phenomenon, as if to imply that here is an important and universal symbolic truth that Jesus was demonstrating in his capacity to bear intolerable pain and come through it to a new beginning. The seemingly impossible can be made possible, even if it might require an earthquake and an angel to assist us. Angels, I am discovering, come in many forms, and profound emotional change can sometimes have the quality of an earthquake about it. At those times it is important to trust in forces external to ourselves and know that a healing process is in motion, which if we can co-operate with it can be the means of our own particular new beginning. Very often it is our anger and the energy it holds that serves as the catalyst for change.

Anything that is alive is constantly changing and evolving as even a quick glance to the garden will confirm. The same is true of the creative process within each of us, unless we consciously or otherwise block it. Very often it will be our anger which will signal to us what needs attending to. It serves as the warning indicator that all is not well, and if we listen to ourselves, our inner wisdom will communicate why we are feeling as we do and what it is about. Maybe something about the current situation resonates on something similar further back in our lives, maybe we feel overlooked or ignored or put upon, whatever it is, by listening to what we are feeling we have the opportunity to do something about it. That's being creative. That's saying, I'm not happy with this situation, something needs to change, what could I do that will make a difference? The answer may not come immediately – it rarely does – but if we are prepared to wait and listen, the opportunity usually presents itself in time. Most of the great reformers were people who were unhappy about a situation, and it made them sufficiently angry to channel all that energy into bringing about change. This lies at the heart of reforms anywhere and is no less significant and relevant in the changes that we need to make in our own situations and within ourselves. Anger is, after all, a response to something. How we respond is up to us. Ignore it and nothing changes anywhere. Use it and a whole new world can potentially open up before us.

People in touch with their anger and the creative life force that it holds quite literally come alive in new and exciting ways. There is a sense of life and vitality about them which is invigorating and intoxicating. They look different, they feel different and they are fun to be with because they are so wonderfully and vibrantly alive. This is in stark contrast to the terrible sterility and apparent deadness of those who, as yet, have been unable to tap into this wonderful life-giving force within themselves. I say 'apparent' because I believe the wellsprings of life reside in all of us, but in some people the wellsprings have become buried beneath layer upon layer of denied feelings, usually because for some reason or another having feelings was experienced as very dangerous and it became less painful not to feel. But although that might initially solve one lot of problems, it creates others, as it is our feelings that are the gateway to life – inner life, that is. The outcome of denying and burying our feelings is to deaden us. We quite literally kill off life and vitality, so that whilst we may have little fluctuation of emotion and give the appearance of being on an even keel, inside there may be a feeling of intense boredom about life. There may be no agonies but no ecstasy either. In this state it could be said that we are entombed in the way I was thinking about earlier. Suspended between life and death. Traumatised and hurt by the past, but too frightened to embrace a future that could give life. It is a most dreadful place to be, if we choose to stay there.

When we get caught up in these kinds of states, we can be both deadly and deadening to be with. For example, which of us cannot admit to having killed off either our own or another's creativity by pouring cold water on a fresh idea, or casting doubt on the enthusiastic decision to do something different? Any and every fresh thought seems to be strangled at conception, which ensures nothing new will ever be allowed to gestate and be brought into life in its own time. The hallmark of this state, which is the fruit of deep and pervasive fear – is sameness. Keep everything the same. Difference is perceived as enormously threatening and frightening. In situations where this way of being has become especially marked, it can be difficult to spend much time in such a person's company, because of the deadening affect that gets generated, and the sense that all creative thought will be stifled. To cut oneself off from this source of creativity is to metaphorically strangle oneself, with obviously disastrous consequences. I wonder if this is something of what Jesus was implying when he talked about sin against the Holy Spirit in Luke 12:10? The Spirit is the essence of that life-giving vibrant force, available and accessible to us all, to increasingly give us the 'life in all its fullness' that Jesus spoke about. However, if we persistently block ourselves off from that life-giving force, we block the potential that could develop in us. I find that a rather challenging thought to reflect further upon.

As I pointed out earlier, all of us have this destructive potential within us to some degree, because its genesis lies in our early experience when it may be that terror was the order of the day and sameness provided some semblance of security in a very terrifying world. After all, it is only the secure child who dares to risk leaving close proximity to mother in order to crawl further afield and explore, trying out new things as a way of discovering what's out there. The anxious child will cling to the familiar for dear life, establishing a pattern that may continue for many years. Such a person learns not to be curious, let alone independent, and resists fiercely any suggestion of such things. Hence their inability to tolerate creativity in others, because creativity by its very nature is about something new and different taking the place of the known, which now feels outgrown. It illustrates again something that I have spoken of several times, whereby we usually only feel comfortable relating to others in those areas which we feel comfortable about within ourselves. This is why the focus of change is always primarily within ourselves, and then from that position, like ripples in a pond, the changes radiate out towards other people and situations. We cannot change others, but we might have an influence.

Trying to change others is always futile, but is especially so without attending to whatever needs to be changed within ourselves first. It is the kind of circumstance that propels fundamentalist endeavours. Fanaticism is at heart an attempt to assuage the doubts within oneself. Sadly religion can sometimes be a forum for this kind of behaviour, where independent thought and independence is perceived to be very threatening, because unconsciously, the changes at a deep level within oneself are detected by others who begin to realise that there is more than one way of seeing things. They may also observe that you have discovered a freedom of thought they want but that they are too frightened to think about for themselves. So their efforts to proselytise and convince get stronger and stronger, which are really their attempts to convince themselves that they are right. Whenever this dynamic is operating within any of us, we become irrationally angry when challenged in any way that suggests our beliefs in that particular area are built on sinking sand rather than the firm ground of conviction, born from rigorous thought that can test and weigh new ideas and see what fits. The late priest HA Williams comments on this propensity with reference to reactions regarding the meaning of the teaching of Jesus, when he likened the Kingdom of Heaven to the merchant man searching for a particular pearl. He writes:

> Jesus said that the Kingdom of Heaven was like this merchant man. At the very least this means that the Kingdom is not something that can be immediately presented to you on a plate, so that all you have to do is to put it into your pocket and feel good. You will find many devout Christians who have forgotten what Jesus said and who will present the Kingdom of Heaven to you in exactly this way. It means, they will tell you, adhesion to a given form of doctrinal orthodoxy. Believe this, that, and the other, and there, you've got the Kingdom. But you haven't got it. All you've got is an excuse to stop looking for it. You may commend the views you have thus accepted with passionate earnestness and zeal, but these may only show that deep down you are afraid that you have been fobbed off with an artificial pearl. All fanaticism is a strategy to prevent doubt from becoming conscious.[(i)]

Having discovered for oneself what one believes, rather than swallowing wholesale what someone else has decided is the truth, is very different to being trapped into a belief system that can't ever be challenged and possibly reappraised. For any of us, as we grow and develop it is inevitable that our ways of thinking also expand and develop. I believe it is when such openness to new thought is vigorously defended against that any of us will feel trapped. It is this sense of entrapment that is a major factor in the pervasive anger that can infiltrate any individual, community or family, religious or otherwise, that takes the stance of dictating what others should believe. When we have discovered for ourselves what we think and believe about particular experiences, we no longer need to defend them so fiercely because they are our own, from the wellsprings of truth within ourselves, and therefore cannot be taken. They may well be subject to attack from the old guard, and it may be that for a time we have to avoid certain places and communities until the new changes within ourselves are sufficiently grounded to withstand the pressures from others, who perhaps see things differently. A newly recovering alcoholic would be sensible to think twice before meeting up with mates in the pub, aware that the pressure to go back into old ways of being might be difficult to resist in that context. Why put oneself under that kind of pressure?

Change of this degree can initially leave a person feeling very vulnerable if all their lives they have simply swallowed wholesale what others think and complied with what others tell them to do. Freedom and independence are costly acquisitions, rarely gained without a shot being fired. Whilst attack from others may be a problem, the greatest attack is usually from within ourselves, from that part of our psyche that wants to hold us back, that wants to preserve the status quo, that causes us to doubt the validity of our own thought when it is different to the prevailing group we belong to. Doubting oneself can be corrosively undermining, as the Biblical story of Peter walking on the water reminds us.[70] You may recall he began this new venture with confidence but once he doubted his ability to see it through, he began to panic and sink. It requires psychological maturity to be able to hold with conviction our own beliefs and opinions, and even more to allow them to be seen; to nail ones' colours to the mast, as it were!

It is the sabotaging quality of this inner dictator that very often causes the greatest destructiveness and setback to personal growth and achievement. You may be quite sure that any new achievement will be subject to this internal attack until we are able to more readily recognise its function and dismiss it, rather than being terrified and captivated by it. A large part of any therapeutic work is often needed to be done in this area if lasting change is to occur and become consolidated. Change of the kind of which I am thinking requires a great deal of support. There is no quick fix in this area.

As we saw in the previous chapter, angry people are very often envious, even if this is as yet not conscious. It comes out in the barbed comments that have an attacking quality about them, which serves to undermine the other person. You see it in the denigrating remarks made of another's achievement, or the remark that rubbishes the other in some way, or the more flagrant destructiveness that deliberately spoils what someone else has, as if to say 'if I can't have it neither will you'. All of these methods highlight the destructive elements of envy which we thought about in some depth earlier. But envy doesn't have to be destructive. There is also a very creative side to it which we often overlook.

We usually only envy something that we admire and would like for ourselves, so in that sense envy can be a springboard to achievement. It can provide a positive role model – but only when we have reached a developmental level within ourselves whereby we are able to recognise that there can be a mutuality about having good things. In other words, it doesn't have to be at the expense of someone else, which is how early infantile envy from the infant part of ourselves experiences everything. At that stage in our lives it is very much a case of either mother has it or the baby has it. The infant at the stage I am thinking of hasn't yet developed the capacity to realise mother (and her derivatives throughout life), can have good things which are not at the expense of me but in tandem with me and separate to me. This second option is in stark contrast to the black and white world of infantile envy which sees everything in absolutes. Either you have it or I have it, which then of course sets up all the rivalry and competitiveness so familiar in relationships. Who has not experienced the triumph associated with acquiring the coveted thing and the wish to flaunt it, as if its acquisition is a major prize to be paraded before all and sundry? Sadly the triumph seems to be the prize rather than the enjoyment of the new thing. All the energy goes into flaunting rather than enjoying.

Envy, when it is operating destructively, precludes enjoyment. How can you enjoy something when all your resources have to be garrisoned to hold onto whatever has been acquired in a defensive, protective kind of way in order to flaunt it – which is as much about flaunting it to oneself as to others, as if to say 'see, look what I've got!' When envy is operating within us, we find ourselves wanting to impress however subtly we might try to cover it over. That is the diet we feed off when we are in the grip of envy, but of course it is an empty diet and sooner or later leaves us feeling deflated. We feel cheated once again, and therefore angry, not least with ourselves for having been conned, and having bought into conning ourselves. The good thing cannot as yet be enjoyed for itself without the need to flaunt, parade or in any other way try and triumph over the other.

But what about the creative aspects of envy? When we are able to recognise that those same resources which one perceived as only residing in others, are also residing in oneself? Then the whole world is our oyster! It may require a considerable amount of time and effort, rather like the merchant man of the gospel story, searching for the particular pearl that he wanted. But the whole point is that by being willing to search, rather than expecting someone else to do the work, and hand it to him, he had the immense satisfaction of finding that for which he was searching, not to mention all the discoveries he made en route. The potential for new things and new experiences is infinite, as all the great composers and innovators down through the ages have proved true again and again, and as we ourselves know when we have felt creative and come up with a bright idea. The human mind is capable of great genius when we are able to work in harmony with it. The story is told of how Robert Louis Stevenson relied upon the wisdom of his inner creative powers to evolve stories for him while he slept; 'This was particularly so when funds were at a low ebb and he needed something marketable and profitable.'[71]

In order for the new thought to be born, there has to be the creative intercourse within ourselves that allows for something new to be conceived and gestated, until such time as it is ready to be born. The period from conception to birth is a variable that ranges from hours and days, to months or years. The same is true of creativity. We have to be able to wait expectantly, rather like a pregnant woman, until that which is conceived within us has grown sufficiently to be ready to emerge and take on a life of its own. This ability to wait is crucial and may well be a capacity we need to develop, for always between conception and germination is the period of waiting. This leads us to think about the link between creativity and sexuality, and their relation to anger.

## NOTES

[64] David Attenborough, *The Private Life of Plants*, BBC Books, 1995, p.193

[65] Sister Kirsty, *The Choice*, Hodder, 1982, pp.157/158

[66] William Blake, *A Poison Tree*, taken from *William Blake's Writings*, edited by GE Bentley Jr, Clarendon Press, Oxford, 1978

[67] Margaret Magdalen CSMV, *Transformed by Love*, Darton, Longman and Todd, 1989, p.58

[68] Mathew 28:2

[69] HA Williams, *The True Wilderness*, first published by Constable and Co. Ltd, 1965, pp.51/52, and in this edition by Mowbray, 1994

[70] Mathew 14:22–32

[71] Dr Joseph Murphy, *The Power of your Subconscious Mind*, first published in Great Britain by Simon and Schuster, 1988, p.147. Reprinted 1990, 1991, 1992(twice), 1993

## Anger and Sexuality

Anger and sexuality are linked in a creative partnership whereby anger can paradoxically both enhance sexuality, as well as detract from it, if it is unacknowledged and influencing our responses unhelpfully. We use the word sex as an umbrella term that covers everything from our gender to the possibility of deep engagement and temporary merging which sexual intercourse in its fullest meaning implies. We talk about people being attracted to each other, which conveys the sense of sexual current facilitating intimacy. Sex implies a coming together but also the need to separate and re-establish our own separate identities, a concept so necessary for healthy sexuality. Couples that feel they have to do everything together, always, can paradoxically stifle the very closeness they are wanting to sustain. Sexuality facilitates people coming to life and allows something new to be created, either literally in the creation of a baby, or in enriching the relationship with the loved other. At the very least, enjoyable sex energises, empowers, and invigorates. Not for nothing do we use the term making love. Loving, when there is a sense of mutual acceptance, is a very renewing experience. How can it not be when so much life-giving energy and current are being mobilised? We are being affirmed in our own identities. This is the creative side of anger, facilitating intimacy at its most profound level.

There is for the person who is comfortable with their aggressive feelings more of a capacity to express likes and dislikes, more of a sense of choice about whether one wants to engage with sexual arousal or not, rather than feeling compelled by oughts and shoulds. Suppress all that potential by denying anger and it's not difficult to see the repercussions that could follow in the area of our sexuality. Blocked anger very often blocks our sexuality in some way. It loses something of the spontaneity that allows sexual feelings to be meaningful, and becomes instead a kind of trying to do the right thing. This has all the hallmarks of duty about it, which as we will all know is the death knell to sexual creativity.

Perhaps we need to go back to our earliest beginnings, when as infants our first sexual (by which I mean erotic) relationship is with our mothers or primary care-givers. If for whatever reason that relationship was in difficulty, then elements of that difficulty, and our feelings about it, will very likely reappear in our adult sexual relationships, based upon that accumulated first experience. It becomes a prototype for what intimacy means for us. Of course, it needs to be remembered that we will each have our own unique experience and understanding of that intimacy, so that what it might mean for me will be different to what it might mean for you. Put that combination together within two lovers and it is not surprising that sex and sexuality becomes a rich breeding ground for conflicts and difficulties. Feelings associated with our earliest infantile experiences of intimacy are not consciously remembered, but are remembered in that repository of feelings, our unconscious, which whether we like it or not, has a very powerful influence upon us and exerts itself in a variety of ways, as this extract from a paper by the psychoanalyst Enid Balint illustrates;

> One husband and wife always appeared to be very loving and considerate with each other when they were together. The wife seemed most grateful for her husband's help and care – particularly when she had her frequent, but short, bouts of depression. To an outside observer they suited each other very well: and so they did, but not in the way that showed itself. The wife, in fact, was very frightened of possible outbursts of temper, and her husband prevented these by his kindness. But by so doing, he prevented her using herself and overcoming her fears of what her temper might do. This suited her husband, because he was also frightened of violence. Their compulsory love-making consisted mostly of petting: penetration was too frightening for both of them. This suggested that the couple could not be violent sexually either, and that was perhaps one of the reasons why they could not achieve a family. The unconscious communication from the wife to the husband was, 'look after me please, save me from my awful violence'. His answer was 'yes, I will'. So he agreed with her that she needed to be saved from her violence, and this suited him very well too, even though he had to live with a sense of resentment without knowing why.[72]

It can be seen that where there is a shared fear of, in this context, anger, it has its impact on our couple relationships. Too much niceness, as we have seen earlier, is not helpful. The endlessly helpful partner might well be perceived as infuriating, not least because all creativity in the sense of creative intercourse, both in dialogue and sexually, gets impaired. It is difficult to be angry with someone who is being so accommodating and kind. But the effect of such behaviour can be to arouse feelings of being stifled – which in other parlance could be said to leave one feeling castrated. It is not difficult to see how anger, or the lack of it, has a direct impact on sexuality. Very often the absence of a sexual relationship between couples is linked to feelings about anger and aggressive instincts, which haven't been able to be spoken about. They, like sex, become taboo. So if you like, between the couple is an unconscious agreement, 'we will not speak about this'. Precisely because the situation is not conscious, the impasse persists, and will do forever unless one or other of them feels able to bring the forbidden subject out into the open. We need to be aware that change within one partner will very likely have an impact on the other, because of the changed unconscious communications. It was Freud who wrote in his paper *The Unconscious*, 'It is a very remarkable thing that the unconscious of one human being can react upon that of another, without passing through the conscious... descriptively speaking, the fact is incontestable.'[73]

Sexuality is about the essence of who we are and how we express ourselves. If we cannot comfortably express our feelings, it is bound to have an affect on how we express, or not, our sexuality; the way we walk, the way we talk, the way we look. These and much more are all expressions of who and what we are, and our anger is a rich source of the energy and current that holds the potential for so much life and vibrancy. It is also a source of the sparkle of being in love – though we have to distinguish between the almost intoxicating feelings associated with apparently having found the right one and the more realistic relationship that develops as a result of being able to embrace our earthiness and basic humanity. This is when we discover, as Warren Colman puts it, 'the capacity to allow the opposites to come together inside the self in the inner world, in all the creative tension of an internal marriage.'[74]

Please note his use of the words 'creative tension'. For many of us the realisation of the paucity of our capacity to tolerate the union of opposites only really comes to light when we enter into a committed relationship, whether or not we formalise it in marriage. The essential feature is the capacity for a true marriage, by which I mean our internal capacity to manage the tension of opposites. Can that be managed creatively, or is the fear that differences of opinion will shatter the relationship? We can all make do or put up with elements that we find unsatisfying for a certain length of time, but such martyrdom generates anger, which if it cannot be allowed for, can only adversely affect the intimacy between a couple and therefore the sexual intimacy. The unexpressed resentment gets expressed sexually in withholding, loss of interest, sadistic remarks, etc. The possibilities for anger to find expression unhelpfully in this arena is endless – possibly because it is an area that arouses such strong feelings anyway.

Of course, unconscious forces are very instrumental in what draws a couple together in the first place, in that instinctive finding of one with the other. We speak of it as the couple fit, by which we mean that within both partners are similar resonances from earlier developmental experiences, but probably they have each developed different ways of managing them. For example they may both have a fear of anger, absorbed from their first families, but one will have been used unconsciously by the family as a repository for that particular emotion, whilst the partner may have used a sibling to carry this emotion and will therefore unconsciously be searching for a mate who is equipped to fulfil that function. Not difficult to see how A is ideally suited to fit with B who has never had to learn how to manage, in this context, angry and aggressive feelings. Trouble comes if one partner decides they no longer wish to carry a particular unconscious role, or cannot, because their emotional bucket is full and itself overflowing. The resentment associated with this state of affairs might then get expressed as a symptom in the very intimate area of their sexual relationship. You can be fairly sure that where there is a problem with intimacy, it will present itself in difficulties to do with sex , which is, we need to remember, about making love. Love-making needs to be about enjoyment of one with the other, rather than a battle-ground for unresolved difficulties. But with the best will in the world, precisely because it arouses such emotive feelings, this area is destined to be the focus for all sorts, serving as the symptom carrier for a difficulty within the total relationship. Unconscious forces carrying unresolved unconscious conflicts are very much stronger than mere good intent, as the following example illustrates;

> Mr and Mrs A had been together for six years when they came for couple psychotherapy. The presenting problem was that their sexual relationship had all but ceased about a year earlier. The overt picture was of a husband who expressed a desire for sex and intimacy, and of a wife who constantly refused him. A few months into the therapy, Mrs A reported that a few evenings earlier they had gone out to dinner, had had a good evening, including a couple of bottles of wine, and on returning home she had seduced her husband. They had had exciting and mutually satisfying sexual intercourse. Mrs A went on to say that she was now feeling very confused and angry, because since that evening her husband had made no sexual approaches to her and had deflected her approaches toward him. Mr A was looking rather shocked and in a panic. He turned to his wife and said rather plaintively that he was very busy at work with a very demanding and important project and just had no energy left at the end of the day.
> 
> The marital couple had unconsciously developed a collusive system that enabled them both to avoid whatever it was that sexual intimacy meant for them. As long as Mrs A refused his sexual advances, Mr A freely made them, knowing that he would be refused. Mrs A unconsciously knew that once she started to make sexual advances to her husband, he could be depended upon to withdraw his sexual interest from her. Between them they ensured that sexual intimacy was avoided, with the overtly defensive behaviour only needing to be enacted by one of them on behalf of both.
> 
> It emerged that for both Mr and Mrs A the avoided relationship was that of a sexual relationship that resulted in the birth of a child. For both of them during early childhood the birth of a child had coincided with loss – in particular the loss of

> attention of the parent of the opposite sex. Mrs A's father had left just after her birth, and then her substitute father left and had a child by another woman. For Mr A the birth of his siblings coincided with the loss of the sole attention of his mother and aunts and of his original home.
>
> For this couple then, the required relationship or shared defensive behaviour, was that of a non-sexual relationship. The avoided relationship was that of procreative sexuality. And the shared fantasy or feared calamity was that if they were to produce a child, the other would leave them, either physically or emotionally. Paradoxically, it was as if, in fantasy, procreative sexuality was life-threatening rather than life-creating.
>
> However, the choice of each other as partners – their unconscious contract – was based on unconsciously recognised mutual anxieties and conflicts. Both unconsciously recognised in the other a shared developmental task: to trust that they could engage in procreative sexuality, produce a child, and not lose the love of a partner.[75]

I have quoted this example at length as it illustrates the complex processes that are around in couple relationships, and that things are not always what they seem. It also illustrates that our choice of partner, in addition to unconscious selection, provides exactly what we each need to help us grow and achieve developmental tasks that remain unfinished and therefore unresolved. However, for this to happen we need to have a freedom of speech to say what we feel and share how we think, along with a willingness to find a solution together if there is to be a meaningful future in a dynamic relationship. The British Telecom slogan 'It's good to talk' has much to commend it!

Intimacy is deepened, and the corresponding enjoyment of what it means to be a couple, considerably enhanced. This capacity to enjoy and be enjoyed will inevitably influence sexual experiences, fostering a greater sense of connectedness. We experience that blissful union of souls in the shared experience of having felt heard and understood, which is often the prelude to sexual intercourse, the culmination of which is the merged state of one-ness when for a time we re-experience the infant bliss associated with being merged with Mother. No wonder we describe this as orgasmic. Maybe we need to reconnect with this early experience, and allow it to remind us and possibly re-mind us, as we allow a different adult experience to inform our accumulated emotional memories about these things. It is not difficult to see that if for any of us our womb experiences or early neonate experiences were clouded in some way, that sex can then become not a good experience, but a reminder unconsciously of something that caused us pain. If we can find the courage to work through the unresolved feelings connected with these early experiences, then it is possible for sex to become not a repetition but a renewing resource that replenishes, precisely because it is different to that early experience, rather than the same. Not for nothing the Biblical injunction that there needs to be a leaving of parents before there can be any hope of cleaving to one's partner.[76] This whole business of attachment is beyond the remit of this book, but very simplified, we cannot genuinely emotionally attach to a spouse or partner if we are still emotionally attached to our parents, and that kind of separation, bound up in the biblical notion of leaving, is a huge issue for any of us, though will likely cause more difficulties for some than others. Depending on what the whole concept of separating from our parents means for us – emotionally, that is. Intellectually it may well be a concept we agree with wholeheartedly, but emotionally we discover the complexity of our inner lives when we embark on the all important process of separating out, to become truly and fully ourselves.

Sexual experience is more likely to be fulfilling if we can comfortably accept and value each others' differences. Otherwise sex becomes another area to exercise control, with all the resentment and anger which that generates. Heterosexual intercourse reminds us in a particularly concrete way that we are different. In making male and female, it is as if God ordained that we should constantly be reminded of the value of difference, and its creative potential.

Sex, at its simplest, is about two people coming together and connecting at a very deep level. A creative duo of opposites. It is this coming together and the potential for creativity as a result of that coming together that I want to think about in this chapter. The sexual relationship symbolises a very profound truth, that just as in order to create a baby, a man and a woman unite and temporarily become one in order that a new life may be conceived, so in the psychic realm there has to be a coming together of opposites, to facilitate the birth of something new, whether it be a new thought, a fresh insight, a new idea that changes the way we think about something, or any other creative happening of which the possibilities are endless.

It is stating the obvious to say that a man and a woman are different, but I state it to underline that it is the capacity to value difference that is tied up in our ability to be creative. Sex can be seen as a celebration of difference. Communities and individuals who, from their own internal difficulties find difference very threatening, try to maintain the status quo by encouraging sameness, thereby ending up strangling the very creativity that could deliver them from the boredom and unhappiness that shapes so much of their lives. In a world where nature is all the time demonstrating to us that difference and creativity go together, it seems strange that in our emotional worlds we seem to find it, at times, hard to follow Nature's example and learn from her quiet but powerful display.

Things do not stay the same, elements fluctuate, seasons come and go, plants take on a life of their own and celebrate their individuality in their own way, co-existing alongside other species that are different. Their unique contribution adds so much to the depth and quality of the total picture. It is this capacity to celebrate our unique differences that is embodied in our sexuality. What it means for me to be me, and you to be you. There is a saying: 'all sunshine creates a desert', indicating something of the sterility and arid quality of sameness. In contrast there is another saying, 'variety is the spice of life', intimating that difference adds a spice to life. We speak of adding spices to food to make it less bland, or add to its piquance, or even to give it a particular culinary distinctiveness and national identity, as when we create Indian, Chinese or Mexican dishes. In other words we give it an identity of its own, all of which conveys something of much greater substance and definition and adds to our capacity for enjoyment of the world around us.

Sex is, at the very least, as I said earlier, a celebration of difference, an enjoyment of our differences without being threatened by them. It is this celebration of difference that contributes so much to the energising quality of a vibrant sexual relationship. Looked at in a symbolic way, the sexual relationship forms a kind of prototype for creativity, with the coming together of opposites as a prerequisite for the birth of something new. It is the new thought that emerges out of conversation with another, the creative idea that is born when heads meet round the boardroom table, the seed-thought that is germinated when we read something that connects with receptive parts of ourselves, and allows a whole new train of thought to arise. In all these examples there has been a coming together, an intercourse with difference that has facilitated something new to be created. Creativity is exciting. We have burst the boundaries of the known and familiar and moved into new territory. Our minds are being expanded. We speak of people getting carried away with a bright idea. There is the energy of the creative union, and the subsequent birth of the new idea.

Where anger in any form is stifled and suppressed there is very often a corresponding stifling of anything that is life-giving, life-enhancing and lively. This stifling is what we do within ourselves when we deny the life-giving potency of anger, and of course for any of us, what we are is what we generate in the vibes around us. The sage of Proverbs knew this truth when he wrote 'As a man thinks, so is he.'[77] The person who is full of life is very alive and lively. They walk into a room and we say the place comes to life, in stark contrast to another person, for whom perhaps too much creativity and life has been stifled. They have the effect of suppressing life. The room goes quiet, conversation becomes stilted and an effort, and before very long one begins to feel very dead.

Doubtless we can all recall situations that illustrate what I am saying. With the former there is a freedom to be ourselves, to say what we think and feel, and know that is very much okay. We feel energised and alive, and speak of coming alive in their presence, suggesting that something about their vitality is infectious. This contrasts with those who for one reason or another, have been unable to be in relation with the wellsprings of life within them.

To deny oneself life, however unconscious that may be, is bound to generate strong feelings of resentment, which, because it isn't allowed to find expression, all gets buried, further suppressing life with every unit of resentment that gets pushed down. There is often a sense that this conversation or that is taboo and in that person's company we end up having to think what to talk about rather than just going with the flow, with the concomitant tension and awkwardness such a situation inevitably creates. Not surprisingly when any of us are in the grip of subjects 'in the forbidden zone' it will inevitably cause us to be compliant and passive, as part of fitting in and not causing trouble or upsetting anyone. Ironically, excessive compliance does upset people, as it has the effect of irritating, and on occasions, infuriating those around them. They of course remain unruffled and unaware. In that psychic interaction an exchange has occurred whereby others 'carry' their anger, leaving the person who has managed to get rid of it free to carry on without it, but impoverished as a result. The highest price that is paid is the loss of vitality and life which gets buried along with their anger. Passivity is the end result of having blocked off so much life-giving energy in burying anger, and sadly, whilst such a mechanism relieves them of a feeling they are not comfortable with, it also deprives them of an emotion that could add so much to the overall quality of their lives.

Anger brings colour to life. It is not without significance that red is often associated with anger, being a very passionate colour, rich and deep, with a distinctive identity of its own. Red roses are associated with lovers, red hearts feature strongly on Valentine's Day. We have the phrase 'red rag to a bull', which indicates something of the passion associated with strong feelings. There is something very robust about red, as there is about anger. People who are able to use their anger creatively have a robustness about them. You are left in no doubt about what they feel and there is a corresponding freedom to just be oneself in their presence, in stark contrast to where that capacity is as yet undeveloped.

Sexuality is one expression of what it means for each of us to be fully ourselves. In that sense therefore it holds the potential to be a celebration of life. In all the myriad ways each of us have, we are saying 'this is me, and it feels good to be me'. When we can have even moments of feeling genuinely excited about our unique value and purpose, we are in touch with our sexuality. We all know that on days when we feel less than our best, it does affect how we feel about ourselves and therefore how we present ourselves to the world. If for various reasons a person has learnt to switch off all expressions of anger, which is the carrier of life-giving energy, it is not surprising that they often end up being very bland people, colourless souls that blend into whatever environment they are in, latching on to the creative ideas of others but unable to access their own creativity. For any of us, when we deny this resource, we deny ourselves life. In the short term it may ensure nothing rocks the boat, that no one is upset, but in the longer term it spells trouble, killing off vitality and all that keeps relationships alive and healthy. It is a very high price to pay for a quiet life. Not least because underneath this apparently unruffled surface lie currents of emotion that can erupt with a frightening intensity.

Our anger is the spark that fuels life. Sparks may fly on occasion, but how often is that not the beginning of something creative happening within a relationship? Real feelings are finally being expressed rather than all this pseudo-niceness that is such a killer and hides a multitude of rather more robust feelings beneath its placid exterior. I'm no mechanic but from observation I have discovered that spark plugs are essential to bring an engine into life. The analogy speaks clearly of the function anger can serve in our lives.

All of this killing off of the life force within us is bound to have an effect on our sexuality, because our minds and bodies are inextricably linked. In the realm of feelings we cannot pick and choose; shut off one and it has an impact on the others, a sort of knock-on domino effect. Emotions and feelings are the tools of relationship and when we choose, usually unconsciously, to keep certain tools out of bounds, either because we are unfamiliar with them or they are deemed too dangerous, we are impoverished in some way. It means we are having to operate on a limited selection of emotional tools. For some this can be very limited, which restricts the user, often in very unhelpful ways. How can you express yourself freely when whole areas of emotional relating are out of bounds and deemed too dangerous?

Sexuality and its expression is about freedom to be who we are and enjoy being that person. For any of us, if we have had to hide behind a particular persona, it can be puzzling to know who we are, with the result that we end up behaving more like chameleons, accommodating to the particular group we find ourselves in. Chameleons, as is well-known, change colour to adapt and blend into their environment as a camouflage against being seen. The problem for us as adults adopting this way of being in the world is that unlike the chameleon we are unable to revert to our true selves. It requires a great deal of internal work to uncover the wellsprings of life that have got submerged beneath years of fitting in and complying. Whilst anyone is caught in the grip of compliant behaviour it is too frightening to have an opinion, and therefore making choices on their own rather than copying other people becomes extremely difficult and stressful. An immediate example that comes to mind is choosing food from the menu at a restaurant. Even those of us who like to think we know who we are can recollect occasions when we have waited to see what others choose, and then based our decision on that.

It is the coming together of opposites that fosters creativity and which the sexual encounter embodies. Every sexual experience is an affirmation of this truth, a reminder to us of our unique differences, which when they meet facilitate the possibility for something very creative to occur, whether literally, in the creation of a baby or metaphorically, in the creativeness of dynamic relatedness. Relationships that are alive will of necessity be changing, because growth implies change. People who want everything to stay the same unwittingly strangle the very life that could rejuvenate a relationship which has perhaps become stale. Nothing has changed. Everything is always done in exactly the same way, which may not be a bad thing in itself but becomes a problem if a partner, spouse or child wants to try something different. The old way of doing things has been outgrown. All parties may be profoundly dissatisfied but unable to communicate how they feel. This impasse seems to be particularly prevalent in the sexual arena, with people putting up with sexual practices they either don't like, don't want, or are bored with, but feel unable to express their true feelings about. The fear is that such openness would hurt the other. The reality is that ultimately we hurt the other far more by not saying anything, because the truth has a way of coming out, even if for years it comes out in disguised ways. It is a measure of our love for another when we can express our true feelings, and a measure of their love for us when they can both accept and acknowledge our feelings, alongside a capacity in sharing their own. Such is the dance of mutuality which lies at the heart of enjoyable sex.

Here as in so many situations that have become lifeless, it is the capacity to externalise our true feelings, including our anger, that can be an important factor in revitalising tired relationships and restoring intimacy or discovering it for the first time. Sparks may fly, but as we have already discovered, it is the spark that's needed to bring an engine into life. The fear for many is that if sparks fly it will be dangerous and destructive – there will be an explosion that devours everything in its vicinity and split the relationship apart irrevocably. It cannot be conceived that there could be a coming together again in dialogue and that something creative could emerge out of honest dialogue.

People who cannot value themselves and their sexuality, find it difficult to feel they are worth investing in, harbouring the erroneous belief that by doing so they are somehow being selfish. Their inability to ask for what they need in their interactions with others, is in effect saying 'I'm not worth anything, don't worry about me, just walk all over me and I won't mind'. What we believe about ourselves gets communicated subliminally, and that is exactly what others do – take us for granted, hardly noticing us. We blend into the background as kind of non-persons, which is not affirming of our unique beauty and individuality. When any of us fall back into compliant ways of being, it very often goes alongside an ability to be very affirming of others, but denigrating towards oneself. Inevitably such a denial of ourselves by ourselves affects how we present ourselves to the world, not least in affecting how confident we feel about our sexuality.

Part of the function of denigrating ourselves is to ensure that we as unique individuals are not seen. The very phrase 'putting yourself down' implies just that. When this mechanism is operating, you may be sure anger is lurking somewhere, even if for a while we may not be aware of it. In order to come to life and refind ourselves, our protest about the situation we find ourselves in will need to be sensitively and understandingly heard; heard primarily by ourselves for ourselves, as we learn to relate more compassionately with the hurting parts of ourselves. I mentioned earlier how it has been said that the greatest betrayal is the betrayal of ourselves, by ourselves. When we deny our authentic true selves, we do ourselves a grave injustice.

Whenever we are out of communication with our true selves, with what we really think, with what we really feel, it is a betrayal of ourselves and does damage. Nelson Mandela in his 1994 inaugural speech had this to say:

> Our deepest fear is not that we are inadequate. Our deepest fear is that we are powerful beyond measure. It is our light, not our darkness that most frightens us. We ask ourselves who am I to be brilliant, gorgeous, talented and fabulous? Actually who are you not to be? You are a child of God. Your playing small doesn't serve the world. There's nothing enlightened about shrinking so that other people don't feel insecure around you. We were born to make manifest the glory of God that is within us. Its not just in some of us: it's in everyone. And as we let our own light shine, we unconsciously give other people permission to do the same. As we are liberated from our own fear, our presence automatically liberates others.[78]

Mr Mandela's words are inspired words that endorse our unique value and worth. When we can really believe it, we are more able to allow our beauty of spirit to be seen and celebrated, rather than, as he put it, shrinking and playing small. That doesn't serve any purpose, least of all for ourselves, and will have profound repercussions on every area of life, including and especially our sexuality. It has to be remembered that this beauty of spirit is potentially in all of us if we can allow it to emerge, nurturing and nourishing it as it does so. Beautiful things need to be valued and cared for, not trampled underfoot and rubbished. The tragedy is that more often than not, it is we ourselves who do the rubbishing. To borrow Nelson Mandela's phrase, 'We were born to make manifest the Glory of God that is within us'. If we really believed that, I'm sure it would make a difference to our self-image. We might even find we can no longer just blindly repeat well-worn prayers and hymns that express the very antithesis of what we have become. We begin to think about what we are saying, as opposed to unthinkingly repeating it. For example, how do you feel about the well-known phrase in the General Thanksgiving that starts by saying 'We your unworthy servants...' Without a doubt such inner growth produces a crisis, when to be true to ourselves means we can no longer just fit in. Of course, that choice is there and we can compliantly say the words, but our integrity will be sacrificed and our bodies may well voice their protest about this betrayal in depressive feelings.

The realisation of the many and varied ways in which all of us from time to time fall into rubbishing ourselves can be very shocking. It comes out in the chance remark, for example when in response to a compliment we say 'it's nothing', it comes out in the way we dress, in our ability to have good things or not as the case may be, in the care we take of ourselves or not. And of course it finds expression in our relationship with our bodies and therefore our sexuality. Can we enjoy our sexuality or is it simply to be tolerated? And what does being a sexual man or woman mean for us? Can we feel good about ourselves, or is there that pervasive sense that we never quite measure up to the usually unrealistic expectations that we might have of ourselves? For most of us these things fluctuate, depending on what is happening for us at any particular time. The words 'good enough', taken from the paediatrician and psychoanalyst DW Winnicott, seem to be a motto that many of us do well to live by.

We need to recognise that few things in life remain constant, and that the expectation of continuous vibrancy, life and energy with no fluctuations is unrealistic and unhelpful. Nature constantly reminds us of the ebb and flow of life with its seasons and periods of creativity balanced with periods of dormancy, when perhaps important things are going on beneath the surface, unseen to the naked eye but essential for the future creativity of the plant. The profusion of daffodils and tulips proudly proclaiming their vibrant colours and embodiment of life in springtime are the outcome of a considerable period of darkness in the soil, to allow changes to go on inside the bulb and without which there would be no creative flowering. We do well to remember that darkness has its place in the life-cycle of creativity. We all share the common experience of being formed in the darkness of the womb, from which all of us have evolved. Creativity needs space and if, in the context of this chapter, our sexuality is to be discovered and allowed to have a life of its own, time needs to be spent getting to know ourselves, our likes and dislikes, the way we tick, what turns us on, what turns us off or, in the wider context of a recurring theme running through this book, what brings us to life and what deadens us?

It is a well-known truism which bears repeating, that each of us can only be comfortable about those things in others with which we are comfortable with in ourselves. Far from being a selfish pursuit which all this getting to know oneself is sometimes criticised for, it actually allows us to give ourselves more fully to others and deepens intimacy. The words of Jesus to 'Love your neighbour as you love yourself' is spot on. The latter however is a lifelong task, the meaning of which unfolds gradually through all the ups and downs of life. We discover, very often, the paucity of our ability to love, particularly our capacity to love ourselves and how this translates in the nitty-gritty of daily life. We are sentient sexual beings and need to celebrate our sexuality and creativity, rather than denigrating or simply tolerating it, if the essence of who and what we are is to be enjoyed rather than endured. Our capacity to live, rather than just exist and get through each day, is one which we can increasingly develop as we first discover and then gradually overcome the elements within our personalities that keep us from embracing life as fully as we might like.

NOTES

[72] Enid Balint, *Unconscious Communications between Husband and Wife*, taken from *Psychotherapy with Couples*, edited by Stanley Ruszczynski, Karnac Books Ltd, 1993, pp.36/37

[73] Freud 1915e, taken from *Psychotherapy with Couples*, Stanley Ruszczynski, Karnac Books Ltd, 1993, p.197

[74] Warren Colman, 'The Individual and the Couple', taken from *Psychotherapy with Couples*, edited by Stanley Ruszczynski, Karnac Books Ltd, 1993, p.132

[75] Stanley Ruszczynski, 'Working with Couples', taken from *Psychotherapy with Couples*, Karnac Books Ltd, 1993, pp.208/9

[76] Genesis 2:24

[77] Proverbs 4:23

[78] Contributed by Lynne Irvine

# *Conclusion*

Volumes can, and have, been written around the vast subject of anger, and much of what has been written here will not necessarily be new. I find for myself it can be helpful to be reminded of certain things again and again, even though I might think I am on familiar territory. It is true that in all probability what has been written may well have a familiar ring about it, but because we are all evolving people, it stands to reason that the more we discover, the more we realise there is yet to be discovered. And just as in the process of writing I have discovered new elements about anger in general, and my own in particular, so it may be for you that there will be thoughts that spark other thoughts. That is the joy of creativity. After all, we are talking about the many faces of anger and therefore it is inevitable that how we view a particular aspect depends very much upon where we're at in ourselves. It may speak with relevance or it may not – or not at the moment, but whatever, I hope it can have widened our understanding of it, and helped us to recognise it as the carrier of a creative life force when we can increasingly harness its life-giving properties. Like good food, it nourishes best when it is fresh. Similarly, dealing with our anger while it is fresh is healthier for us than allowing it to become stale, when it loses its life-giving potential, becoming instead a potential source of trouble, poisoning us in the process.

My hope is that the book can serve as a kind of signpost that can point us in the direction of life – and signposts are there to be used when we need them. What I have written might serve as a catalyst to spark creative thoughts within yourself, thoughts that perhaps have been lying dormant for months or years, just waiting for something that will allow them to germinate and come to life. Sometimes we need permission to feel what we feel and know that is very much okay. There is an old adage that says, 'When the disciple is ready, the teacher appears.'[79]

For any of us, what is it that unconsciously directs us to pick up and read a particular book? I suggest that something within us is receptive and at some level wanting to explore and expand further our thinking on a particular subject. It may be that something of what has been written here finds some kind of an echo within yourself, and in the intercourse between my thoughts and your own there may well be the beginnings of something new developing.

In that sense I believe the conclusion is a very important part of this book, bringing together the various themes that have been written about. Two recurring themes permeate the text. The first is how all through our lives, issues connected with life and death confront us, in terms of whether the way we live leads us increasingly to find life and live it more fully, or whether, often without realising it, we sabotage life by making choices that deaden us and kill off life. The second theme is that the resource for living life or resisting it *resides within us*, and not just some of us, but in all of us. That is the concept that excites me more than any other because it means that the storehouse of possibilities is accessible to us all and not dependant upon fortune, money, brains or geographical location.

One of the factors that unites us is that we all have an inner world, made up of our thoughts, feelings, experiences and images, based upon experiences in our external world. It is the creative dialogue between the two that determines what we make of that raw material we call life. This is why developing the relationship we have with ourselves is so fundamental to the quality of life any of us can experience. It is here within us that change of any kind has to happen and be registered as the proverbial sage knew when he wrote 'Be careful how you think: your life is shaped by your thoughts.'[80] The apparent simplicity of that statement is mind-blowing, particularly when we recognise that for most of us it seems to take the rest of our lives changing our thinking!

It is our thinking that affects our view of the world, which is inevitably coloured by the numerous experiences that make up our lives and which have been encoded in their entirety within us. The joy of having an inner life is that our blueprint for living can continually be updated – and needs to be. This reminds me of a very refreshing article written several years ago by Lionel Blue in *The Tablet* about his experience of the interface between religion and analysis.

> I realised that knowing about God without knowing about yourself could only lead to fanaticism or banality or both (the usual combination); for 'the Kingdom of Heaven is within you'.
>
> There were lots of other bonuses too – not least of which was honesty. Religion ought to be good at that, but is not. It is good at the grander truths on the mystical heights but did not seem to cope very well with the humbler ones on the lower slopes. Those I learnt not on my knees but horizontal on my couch. I suppose in formal religion there is just too much role-playing. The psycho stuff also taught me to listen, whereas at my seminary I learnt to preach and talk; and I tried to hear people's real questions (usually not the ones they first presented). Later on I realised that my answer was not relevant – for the answer to stick they had to find it out for themselves, as I had had to do.
>
> I learnt many other lessons as well. Such as, that the angels and demons I encountered were within me and part of me, and the demons needed more affection and humour than the angels did.
>
> What did religion give to my psycho stuff? It made it possible. Several of us started analysis at the same time, but I was the only one who stuck it to the end. The reason was prayer. You need a lot of courage to face yourself 'without a wardrobe of excuses'. The Holy Spirit – thank God – gave it.[81]

We all get caught up in role-playing, particularly as children when gaining approval is so necessary for survival and early development. But as adults such roles can become constricting and unhelpful, and militate against us rather than for us, stopping us from doing what we need or want to do. They hold us back, which is why in this business of personal growth and our quest to find life, we have to recognise roles for what they are and be willing to gradually let them go as we outgrow the need for them. Easier said than done sometimes, however much we may yearn for this inner freedom to be ourselves. To use Lionel Blue's phrase, 'You need a lot of courage to face yourself without a wardrobe of excuses.' It is a process of becoming. We are all the time evolving into something, becoming more real, more whole –

by which I mean we can tolerate and welcome acceptingly (eventually) our shabby bits as well as our shiny bits. This reminds me of the Velveteen Rabbit, and a particular conversation held between the rabbit and the skin horse in the nursery.

> 'What is *real*?' asked the rabbit one day, when they were lying side by side near the nursery fender, before Nana came to tidy the room. 'Does it mean having things that buzz inside you and a stick-out handle?'
> 'Real isn't how you are made,' said the skin horse. 'It's a thing that happens to you. When a child loves you for a long, long time, not just to play with, but *really* loves you, then you become real.'
> 'Does it all happen at once, like being wound up,' he asked, 'or bit by bit.'
> 'It doesn't happen all at once,' said the skin horse. 'You become. It takes a long time. That's why it doesn't often happen to people who break easily, or who have to be carefully kept. Generally, by the time you are *real* most of your hair has been loved off, and your eyes drop out, and you get loose in the joints and very shabby.'[82]

'Real isn't how you are made… It's a thing that happens to you.' That is a process and, as the skin horse so wisely said, 'You become. It takes a long time.' But, as every artist knows, the colours on the canvas can be changed and modified at will. We each create our own picture, and the enjoyment of this kind of creativity is that our lives are a canvas in the making. The darker colours give depth, the light is only meaningful in proximity to the existence of its shadow, and of course the picture that is created only portrays the image as it is perceived at that time. Inevitably at a different time and from a different perspective what we see may well be portrayed very differently. Hence the title of this book, *Faces of Anger*, which has been a reflection on various perspectives to enlarge our understanding of anger, and see it more as an ally than an enemy.

Anger and life are very much connected. If you like, anger is the oxygen of life. Deny it access and before very long you have lost your connection to the wellsprings of life within yourself. Emotional vitality is sacrificed for an emotional sterility that masks as life, but is in fact a counterfeit, and why make do with a fake when you can have the real thing? As Jesus once commented in the insightful way He had, 'would any of you who are fathers give your son a stone when he asks for bread?' And perhaps even more to the point 'or would you give him a snake when he asks for bread?'[83] Rhetorical questions that we do well to ponder reflectively about with regard to our own lives. Some of us have made do with stones for far too long when what we have been wanting is bread that satisfies. It is not insignificant that Jesus spoke of being 'the bread of life'[84] implying that satisfaction and nourishment comes from meaningful relationships, rather than religious dogma which sits in our stomachs like a stone and weighs us down.

All too often we impose upon ourselves restrictions and limitations that have more to do with our inability to have and enjoy good things than any spiritual justification. I wonder if part of our dilemma is that we have viewed anger in a very restricted, narrow form, seeing it only as something dangerous and frightening, something that can easily get out of control, and therefore to be avoided at all costs? With this limited view we lose sight of what a resource for living it is, and inadvertently turn our backs on something precious and life-enhancing. How many relationships have died, or at any rate lost their vitality through an inability to process resentment, frustration, annoyance and any of the other feelings that come into anger's remit? Equally, when conflicts can be shared and spoken about, the possibility for relationships to be restored and deepened is present. But of course, to experience the raw emotionality of anger can sometimes be very difficult. It can feel so frightening and life-threatening rather than life-enhancing. Anger and love go together, like the two sides of a coin, but the fear for many is that if anger is allowed it will blow a relationship apart. Explosions may happen from time to time, but all that energy is very often the harbinger of something much more real and robust. This is a truth we have to discover for ourselves, and as Sister Mary Magdalen realised in the example quoted earlier, once isn't enough. Every fresh situation seems to evoke the old fears and demand fresh courage to make of it a creative outcome, until we build up a well of new emotional experiences that help counteract the old templates within us.

One of the functions of creative conflict is that there is a coming together of opposites. Two people come together, opposing sides can talk and understand each other and out of that coming together is the potential for a more dynamic relationship. Sterile relationships may go along on an even keel with never a cross word but they can be very boring and deadly in their lifelessness. Everything remains the same. No challenges, no differences of opinion and therefore not much fun or life either, and little possibility for very much creative to happen. Whenever we fall into idealising someone, we need to ask ourselves what that need to put them on a pedestal is in the service of? Is it to mask our own angry feelings, or our envy of them, is it that if we saw them as ordinary mortals our world of illusory perfection would start to crumble and cause us to have to re-orientate our map of the world?

This is the kind of scenario that underlies some affairs. The relationship has become so boring through an inability to process real feelings together, that one partner ends up finding life and vitality elsewhere. The excitement has to be found outside the relationship, rather than within it. How different it could be if feelings could be shared and processed. But that can be a very frightening prospect for some, if their early experience imbued in them a sense of awkwardness about feelings and their expression. It is not uncommon that the purpose of some affairs is to provide a safe escape into an illusory relationship rather than hammer out the difficulties on the anvil of a real relationship. Affairs can also serve as the metaphorical third leg of a stool, providing stability if the couple feel unbalanced for some reason. What a difference it could make to feel we can each increasingly create the kind of relationship we want, rather than living out a template of inherited expectations about how to relate. However, for this to happen, there has to be the ability to try out different ways of relating, patterns that might and probably will challenge family expectations, with all the potential reverberations that can cause. And the capacity to make space for angry feelings to find expression is likely to bring about the closer relationship we are wanting. It is our ability to process our hurts and frustrations, our needs and longings that can bring life and vitality back into relating that has become lifeless and therefore feels dead. Anger is energy. It is the current and currency of life, that forms a kind of psychological radar system keeping us in touch with how you impact on me and I impact on you.

William Blake (1757–1827) wrote a particularly apposite poem in this context which I quoted in full elsewhere. The simplicity, but also the profundity of the first verse bears repeating:

> I was angry with my friend.
> I told my wrath, my wrath did end.
> I was angry with my foe,
> I told it not, my wrath did grow.[85]

Those words graphically illustrate how unresolved anger grows and ultimately destroys friendship, and equally that it is a true friend with whom it is safe enough to be angry and know that the anger, far from destroying the relationship, usually deepens it. The poet has a way of simplifying this whole anger issue. 'I was angry with my friend, I told my wrath, my wrath did end'.

' We have all known moments when we have felt gloriously and wonderfully alive, and need to nurture and nourish those experiences. Equally we need to listen to the protest of our feelings when we habitually frustrate and deny ourselves those things that bring us to life. Our anger will in one form or another alert us that something somewhere is wrong. It is the energy that our anger generates that propels us to do something about the situation, whether it is on the personal, social or global level. How many times do we not see anger being the catalyst to facilitate political or social change to circumstances that are felt to be intolerable? The abolition of slavery, the overthrowing of communist regimes, the provision of housing for the homeless, the list is endless. Usually these things about which we feel very strongly have their symbolic counterpart within us, so that fixing it for 'them out there' is also at some level fixing it for the enslaved, imprisoned parts of ourselves. Writing this book is no different. The process of writing further helps to clarify and expand my thinking around this subject, which has meaning for me and universal relevance for us all, particularly in these days of wars and rumours of wars. The war needs primarily to be won within ourselves, as we unite the conflicting elements of our own personalities into a more harmonious inner community. This is no soft option, requiring courage and persistence to see it through. What is the alternative – endless bloodshed as internal conflicts get acted out on the world stage?

The themes of life and death have featured regularly over the course of this narrative and are continually replaying in our lives. Significantly, the genesis of this book was conceived on the anniversary of my brother's death, the trauma of which, with all that followed, was the catalyst for increasingly enabling me to find life, and come alive in new ways. But for that to happen, old ways of being that were no longer serving me usefully, had to be allowed to die, and death, in whatever form it comes is painful. We grieve, and discover in the process that our grieving is part of the process of letting go and moving on, a prelude for something new to come into being. Giving birth is in itself a painful process, but the pain loses its grip with the joy of the new life that has been born, and something akin to that process happens every time we allow a thought to germinate and grow until such time as it is ready to be born. We need to remember that the process of giving birth to anything is uniquely personal – and some birth experiences are straightforward, while others are both painful and protracted and require of the mother and midwife that they stay with the process, assisting if necessary but believing all the while that the baby also has its own momentum to be born. That is true of all creativity, if we can wait patiently, trusting in the creative process, which will be born in its own time and in its own way.

Sometimes an element in depressive episodes is that loss in some form or other is being grieved and let go of, in order that something new can be allowed to grow, and be born. Depressive experiences of this kind are no less painful, but ultimately are a sign of something very creative going on inside and need to be allowed to take their course. It is likely that the depression is heralding a new beginning of some kind in the not-too-distant future.

Nature is continually reinforcing this truth to us, that death in some mysterious way can facilitate life. 'A grain of wheat, remains no more than a single grain unless it is dropped into the ground and dies. If it dies, then it produces many grains.'[86] So said Jesus, speaking a universal truth in the picture language of parable on one occasion. A single seed on its own is a very sterile, lifeless thing, but it holds huge potential for creativity and life. However, it will forever remain just a seed unless it is surrounded by conditions conducive to its germination and be allowed to fulfil itself, and have a life of its own.

In order for that to happen, it has to die to what it was – by which we mean that there has to be a separation. The germinated seedling breaks out from its hard casing, becoming vulnerable, and in the process becoming more fully itself, allowing hitherto unimagined life and creativity to emerge. The symbolism in all this imagery needs no translating. When it happens it is a miracle. Our part is to be open to the miracle, and an important part of that openness is a willingness to discover what life and coming alive might mean for us as individuals. For that to happen we have to be willing to let go of what we were, for what we might become, which requires courage to take the risks involved and overcome the fears associated with growth.

The tragedy is that for many, every stirring of their free spirit and spontaneity in their formative years got stamped on and crushed by one means or another, with the result that in order to protect themselves from the feared pain of continually being crushed, a part of them gives up, surrendering their tender free spirit and the seeds of life that go with it. It can take a very long time to overcome the fear, by now deeply embedded, and risk once more breaking out from their protective casing allowing themselves to be seen. The tender seedling, freshly emerging from its outgrown seed case, is very vulnerable and easily destroyed until roots are established and a rather more robust plant develops that can withstand the elements. The tragedy is that the alternative of staying within the apparent safety of the seed case is that all further growth gets stifled, and the person concerned lives out a stunted kind of life, too scared to separate from whatever keeps them trapped in their metaphorical seed case, yet at the same time feeling frustrated by the limitations and restrictions that anything we have outgrown inevitably causes.

Within all of us is hidden potential, seeds of creativity if you like, lying dormant and waiting to be encouraged into germination, with all the promise of new life inherent in that. Allowing our anger to have a life will very often bring us to life in the process. It seems ironic that anger is so often associated with the destructiveness that gives it a bad name. The irony is that anger only becomes so destructive when its life-enhancing potential is blocked. We need to understand that anger is a response to something and a reaction about something, and our task is to discover what it is we are so angry about. Failure to do so means it either gets internalised and makes us ill, or it erupts unhelpfully under pressure in the violent outburst or the attack on people or property, or it gets projected into others for them to act out. Whether outwardly or inwardly, such impotent expressions of anger exact a huge toll, not just on society but on individuals and families, communities and countries, because the cause of the anger has not been addressed in any meaningful and satisfactory way. What a waste of so much energy that could have gone into trying to resolve the conflict rather than generating more.

Staleness and boredom in our relationships are sure signs that communication has broken down. All sunshine makes a desert, we are told, and relationships where there is never a cross word will sooner or later become arid and lifeless. The tragedy is that there are those who see that state of affairs as a virtue to be proud of, not realising that just beneath the surface lie explosive emotions, liable to erupt damagingly because they have been denied expression for so long. Like water in a pipe that has had its outflow blocked, when something happens to shift the blockage, the resulting outpouring spills out all over the place, wasting a precious resource and causing a big mess in the process. More seriously for those for whom all expressions of anger are taboo; it can be like the build up of pressure behind a dam wall. Ultimately unless the pressure is reduced safely through sluice gates, the pressure mounts and in some situations the dam wall holding all that damned up emotion in check gives with disastrous and tragic consequences.

How much better for all concerned that we learn to value and harness this precious emotion, which like rain on parched ground can bring us to life in new and creative ways and allow us increasingly to live fully as ourselves, rather than existing in a shell made up of other peoples' expectations of us, or our own inability to break out from whatever imprisons and restricts us. That applies to us all, as we all carry emotional wounds in varying and differing ways that leave their mark upon us. These are the things that make us uniquely the people we are. That being so does not mean we are doomed to stay a particular emotional shape forever. The question for all of us is whether or not we feel as emotionally alive as we would like? And if not can we discover what keeps us from coming fully alive in increasing measure, and be willing to do the work that meaningful relationships require?

Anger, as we have seen, has many faces, rather like a diamond with its many facets and angles that all reflect light in differing ways depending on which direction you look at it. I referred earlier to anger being like a jewel and want to end this book by affirming that this is a jewel we all have within ourselves. It is not something to be dismissed or ignored or worse still, buried. It is an essential part of our humanity, given to us along with all our other emotions as a resource for living, another tool that we can learn to use, in order to enhance our relationships rather than detract from them. This implies a sense of process and that therefore the work of relationships is ongoing. We might at times escape into illusions of perfection if only we could grasp it, but that is an illusion and as such sets us up to be disappointed.

One of anger's greatest gifts to us, when it is acknowledged and valued, is its capacity to enrich relationships and deepen emotional contact – which ultimately is what gives meaning to life and therefore a greater sense of satisfaction. We connect with one another, and the energy that our anger holds provides the spark to bring the connection to life. When we can access this resource not only do we have more energy for living, but we feel more alive. It is as if the current flows into every cell in our bodies and brings us to life in the process. Block off this emotion and you block the wellsprings of life. Just as blocked anger affects our relationships with one another, so too will it affect our relationship with God.

It seems a terrible tragedy that God, who is the source of our authentic feelings and the creativity that comes from them, can sometimes get lost in 'churchianity', which is what happens when the church gets into 'telling us what to do' mode, deciding what is or isn't appropriate for us and our relationship with God. This is not a new phenomenon. Religion versus spirituality has been a dilemma for every age and era, and Jesus had quite a bit to say to the Pharisees of his day who got lost in the logistics of relationship with God as they perceived it, rather than the experience of the relationship. Incidentally, it also evoked considerable anger in him when vulnerable people were being exploited by the religious authorities of the time, so anger towards the established Church is nothing new! Part of my purpose in writing as I have is to open the door for each of us to discover for ourselves what God means for us as individuals, and find our own way of developing that relationship, which may well differ from what others decide. The important issue is the relationship, not what others think. Only when our true selves feel in harmony with our image of God will our capacity to enjoy God develop. Otherwise we are forever bound to old traditions that conflict with current discoveries. A certain liberating freedom comes when we decide to follow our hearts and be true to the God within us, rather than our heads, which may still be in thrall to established traditions. The Genesis story reminds us that the work of creation was a source of much pleasure to the Creator, and I believe that is no less in the creative work that goes on within us. The process of transformation requires energy, which our anger can supply. It is this appropriately channelled energy residing in all of us which holds the power to transform and renew. It is treasure with limitless potential, waiting to be endlessly discovered and harnessed, but buried treasure is no good to anyone, least of all ourselves. It has to be unearthed and utilised.

I am aware that in writing a book of this kind it can vastly over-simplify issues that are anything but simple. If it were just a matter of reading a book and following a recipe we would all be sorted! The crunch comes at the point where we have to think about what any of this means for us, in the context of our lives, and that can be very difficult and unsettling. How we can or cannot express our anger is a very complex issue and the purpose of this book is to whet the appetite, a sort of aperitif that leaves us hungry for more, which of course is there for the finding. The book of Proverbs has an apposite suggestion for us.

'Drink the water from your own wells,
Fresh water from your own source.'[87]

The joy of reading is that sometimes a particular thought stays with us and leads us to further thoughts of our own which we can then follow to our own conclusions. If that is so the book will have achieved its purpose in being a signpost that points you in a particular direction. Where your path ultimately leads you is one of the joys of journeying. Always there are new horizons that beckon, new discoveries to be made. And throughout, the Spirit of God, who is the source of all creativity and life, joins with the creative spirit within each one of us, leading us into all truth, which I have come to understand is the truth as we experience it for ourselves in the context of our own lives. Second-hand truth is no match for authentic thoughts that we have discovered first hand for ourselves. All too often it has been the wholesale swallowing of what other people think is good for us that has been so death–dealing to that creative life force within us. We have to taste and see, and on that basis decide for ourselves what brings us to life and what deadens us. Our anger will be our ally, informing us when we have taken a wrong turn and encouraging us to change direction.

It may be that thoughts have been stirred as a result of something that has been written, beckoning us to pursue it, rather like a star that stands out from the galaxy. It could be said that something about it catches our eye and makes it stand out for us, as happened for the wise men of old – wise in part because they did follow its guiding light. The psychoanalyst Donald Kalched makes an interesting observation in this context.

> There is something powerful in the human psyche that wants to incarnate, and through a human love strong enough to survive destruction, to be born under the star of its own destiny in a Bethlehem of the Soul. And then there is another force that resists that incarnation – like King Herod in the ancient story

who lives in fear of the new life that wants to enter, and tries to dismember it with every violent power at its disposal.[88]

That excerpt encapsulates the themes in this book of life and death, of forces that are life-giving or death-dealing, and always within all of us there is that constant interplay between the two forces. There are many stars out there shining in their own way, but it may be that one particular star catches our attention in a particular way, beckoning us to venture beneath its guiding light. If we can trust its beckoning light and follow, not necessarily knowing where it will take us, then like the wise men of old we may find it leads us to 'the Bethlehem of our soul' that awaits to receive the new beginning, however humble. Sometimes in our confusion we are unsure where to begin – maybe the wisdom of the Tao can help us, 'The longest journey begins with a single step'.

---

NOTES

[79] Taken from *The Fire Of Silence and Stillness: An Anthology of quotations for the Spiritual Journey*, edited by Paul Harris, Darton, Longman and Todd, 1995, p.142

[80] Proverbs 4:6

[81] Lionel Blue, *Out of the Blue; A little bit of Psychobabble, The Tablet*, 10th December, 1994

[82] M Williams Bianco, *The Velveteen Rabbit*, Heinemann Ltd, London, 1970

[83] Mathew 7:9

[84] John 6:35

[85] From William Blake, 'A Poison Tree', taken from *William Blake's Writings*, edited by GE Bentley Jr, Clarendon Press, Oxford, 1978

[86] John 12:24

[87] Proverbs 5:15

[88] Donald Kalched, *Daimonic Elements in Early Trauma*, paper taken from the *Journal of Analytical Psychology*, Edition 48, no.2, Blackwell Publishers Ltd, April 2003, pp.145–169

Printed in the United Kingdom
by Lightning Source UK Ltd.
102740UKS00001B/85-135